Henry W. Beecher, Benjamin Fiske Barrett

Letters on the Future Life, Addressed to Henry Ward Beecher

Henry W. Beecher, Benjamin Fiske Barrett

Letters on the Future Life, Addressed to Henry Ward Beecher

ISBN/EAN: 9783337143657

Printed in Europe, USA, Canada, Australia, Japan

Cover: Foto ©ninafisch / pixelio.de

More available books at **www.hansebooks.com**

The Future Life.

ON

THE FUTURE LIFE,

ADDRESSED TO

HENRY WARD BEECHER.

BY

B. F. BARRETT.

"There is no Death! What seems so, is transition;
This life of mortal breath
Is but a suburb of the life elysian,
Whose portal we call Death."—LONGFELLOW.

PHILADELPHIA:
CLAXTON, REMSEN & HAFFELFINGER.
1873.

TRANS. TO CENTRAL RESERVE

Entered, according to Act of Congress, in the year 1872, by
CLAXTON, REMSEN & HAFFELFINGER,
in the Office of the Librarian of Congress, at Washington.

STEREOTYPED BY J. FAGAN & SON, PHILADELPHIA.

PREFACE.

THE immediate occasion of these Letters, was Mr. Beecher's sermon on "The Hereafter" published in PLYMOUTH PULPIT, March 23d, 1872. Three of them appeared first in THE GOLDEN AGE; and were favorably received, I am told, by persons of spiritual insight and religious culture.

I have, therefore, been induced to add three more of considerably greater length, and to publish them together in their present form; hoping they may exert some influence in overcoming the still prevalent but senseless prejudice against the seer of Stockholm, and may increase the growing interest in his writings among the reading and thinking classes.

Mr. Beecher says that the "great Future to which we are going"—meaning the world which the soul enters when the body is laid aside—"is now all haze, with here and there a single point jutting out before us." To a large majority of Christians, no doubt it is. But it need not be so. It is not so to that small but steadily increasing band of believers who have become familiar with the writings of the Swedish sage.

The author's aim has been, to show that a veritable revelation of the condition of things in the great Hereafter has actually been vouchsafed, and to vindicate Swedenborg's claim as a divinely authorized seer and revealer of the realities of the spiritual world.

The Letters, though addressed to the esteemed pastor of Plymouth pulpit, are intended for the thoughtful and inquiring of all denominations — and of *no* denomination. The question they undertake to discuss, is one of exceeding interest and importance. And it is hoped the discussion has been conducted in such a spirit, and the argument presented with such force, as to produce a favorable impression upon the candid reader, and lead him ultimately to the crystal light of the New Jerusalem. More than this the author could not ask.

B. F. B.

WEST PHILADELPHIA,
September 1, 1872.

CONTENTS.

I.
MR. BEECHER'S POSITION CRITICALLY EXAMINED 13

II.
SWEDENBORG'S CLAIM—AND CREDIBILITY . . 24

III.
HIS PHILOSOPHY OF SPIRIT-SEEING 37

IV.
VINDICATION OF HIS CLAIM 47
    DEATH AND RESURRECTION 49
    FORM OF THE SPIRIT 53
    MAN ESSENTIALLY A SPIRIT 55
    THE SUN OF HEAVEN 56
    LIGHT AND HEAT IN HEAVEN 57
    OBJECTS SEEN IN HEAVEN 60
    THE ESSENCE OF HEAVEN 62
    MANY SOCIETIES IN HEAVEN 65
    HEAVEN AND THE CHURCH WITHIN THE SOUL . . 67
    THE WHOLE HEAVEN RESEMBLES A MAN . . . 70
    CHANGES OF STATE IN HEAVEN 73
    TIME AND SPACE IN HEAVEN 76
    CORRESPONDENCE OF SPIRITUAL WITH NATURAL THINGS 81
    HOUSES IN HEAVEN 87

	PAGE
Governments in Heaven	91
Temples and Worship in Heaven	93
Speech of the Angels	95
Danger in Speaking with Spirits	99
The Wisdom of the Angels	101
Angelic Innocence	104
Heavenly Peace	106
Angels and Devils from the Human Race	108
A Heaven for Gentiles	110
Children in Heaven	113
Rich and Poor in Heaven	118
Marriages in Heaven	121
Employments in Heaven	128
The Happiness of Heaven	132
The Life that Leads to Heaven	143
The Nature of Hell	147
The Fire of Hell	151
Appearance of the Devils	154
The Lord does not cast into Hell	155
Man's Book of Life	159

V.

NEED AND TENDENCY OF HIS DISCLOSURES . . 164

VI.

COLLATERAL TESTIMONY 176

"THE great question which concerns us all, is that of immortality. Am I near the verge and end of myself? Am I made to tick and keep the hours of this mortal sphere only? When I am done here, shall I be run down forever, never to move again, or record the hours of time? Or do I belong to the horology of the universe? Passing through life, do I enlarge my sphere? Do I fit myself to live more nobly, more fruitfully, with augmented sweep of being?"— *Henry Ward Beecher.*

"An unclouded view of the spiritual world once disclosed, how solemn and yet how entrancing are its perspectives!— and how near they come and open beneath our eye! There is no death, but only the removal of deathly coverings; the word vanishes from the Christian vocabulary, and the thing it represented vanishes from the prospect of the Christian believer. For ourselves, we cannot raise to heaven a song too jubilant for this victory over the grave. All fear of mere death is removed; and that done, we can fix our undisturbed attention upon the only thing to be feared in any state of being,— the moral evil that glooms from within us, and clouds the landscape, and shuts out the smile of God." — *Edmund H. Sears.*

LETTERS

ON

THE FUTURE LIFE.

I.

MR. BEECHER'S POSITION CRITICALLY EXAMINED.

My Dear Brother:—Thirteen years ago, I had occasion to write you some friendly letters on the subject of the Divine Trinity. Your recent sermon on "The Hereafter," which I have just read in *Plymouth Pulpit,* moves me again to address you; and to present some thoughts on this interesting subject which seem to me worthy of your consideration, and which I doubt not you will receive in the same friendly spirit in which they are written. If so, no harm can come from what I say, even though I should fail to impress you with my own convictions. The weak may sometimes aid the strong; and little children, you know, may now and then drop hints from which wiser heads may profit.

For fifteen years or more, I have been an interested reader of nearly all your published writings; and I have often read and loaned and recommended them to others. I have generally found them interesting and instructive —

always pervaded by a free, earnest and catholic spirit, and abounding in the advanced thought of these New Times upon nearly all religious and theological questions. Perhaps you are not aware how closely most of your religious beliefs and teachings resemble those of a great author who is fast coming into notice, but of whose writings the majority of intelligent Christians are still profoundly ignorant.

I mean Emanuel Swedenborg; — a man of rare gifts and attainments, and whose writings furnish evidence, I think, of a higher spiritual enlightenment than was ever enjoyed by any other individual. Upon all the more important and fundamental doctrines of the Christian religion, I find in your teachings substantially the same views as those put forth by the great Swede more than a hundred years ago — widely different, however, from the views commonly recognized as orthodox in Swedenborg's or even in our own times. This statement will, no doubt, surprise your friends — and possibly yourself; nevertheless it is strictly true.

On the central doctrine of Christianity — the Divine Incarnation and true Object of religious worship; on the supreme and sole divinity of Jesus Christ; on the nature and way of regeneration; on men's various conceptions of God and the cause thereof, and how to form right conceptions of Him; on the essential character of the Divine Being as consisting of perfect love and perfect wisdom — of love that is exercised alike toward the evil and the good; on man's capability of becoming somewhat like

God, and *how* we are to grow into the Divine likeness; on love to the Lord and the neighbor as constituting the essential thing in the Christian religion and in every true church — and how to develop and strengthen this love; on the nature of the resurrection and the ministry of angels; on the nature of true and practical religion and how it is to be attained; on the highest kind of worship, as consisting in the conscientious and faithful performance of the duties of one's vocation; on the great end of human existence — to wit, the full and orderly development of all the noblest elements of human character — the development of the man into the angel; on the momentous question of the proper religious education and training of the young; on the importance of social recreation — dancing, games, innocent amusements of all kinds — not only as things to be tolerated by Christians as harmless, but things to be everywhere encouraged as useful; on the breadth and comprehensiveness and catholicity of the Lord's true Church, and the endless variety to be expected therein, as in all the rest of the Creator's works; on forms and ordinances and institutions and rituals, and their comparative insignificance, and utter worthlessness save as means or helps in the formation of heavenly character; — on all these, and many other kindred topics, I generally find you in such substantial agreement with Swedenborg, that I reckon you as one of the most efficient instruments in the propagation of the New Christianity; — all the more efficient from the fact that you have never taken *on* any new name, however you may have shaken *off* the old theology.

But when you come to speak of the life after death, you fall ever so far below my expectations. You fail — please pardon this frankness — to do justice to yourself or your theme. Your discourse is meagre and comparatively barren. You rob death of none of its stings. You throw no cheerful light on that vast realm of being beyond the tomb. Your faith seems weak, your eye-sight dim, your foot-hold insecure. You are far less interesting and instructive than you might be and ought to be. Your discourse lacks power in the degree that your convictions lack clearness and strength. You are, according to your own confession, in such utter darkness concerning the life beyond the grave, that some of your readers may, I fear, be led to doubt whether indeed there *be* any such life. You do not pretend to know what heaven is, or what hell is; what are the joys of the one, or the miseries of the other.

Of course, then, you have no instruction to offer others concerning the state or condition of people in either of these kingdoms in the great Hereafter. You "infer" from the teaching of Christ and some of the apostles, "that we shall retain our identity in the other life; but," you add, "there is no explicit knowledge or teaching on this subject." And how far from *certain* you consider even this, may be inferred from your saying, "that when we come to live together again, much that we call our personal identity here, will be left behind." You do not know but "all the passions and appetites and imperfections"— and sins, I suppose, though you do not say this — will drop off along with the material body, leaving to some of us very little, when we enter the other world, whereby our friends would be able to recognize us. You do not know whether those who die in infancy will remain forever in that diminutive and infantile form, or whether they will grow there to the full stature of manhood and womanhood; though you think "very likely" the latter. You do not know what is the condition of the wicked, any more than of the righteous, in the Hereafter; though you feel constrained to teach on this subject what you find in the Bible (according to the spirit, or the letter?) — adding: "It is there; and if I am faithful to my whole duty I must preach it. As a surgeon does things that are most uncongenial to himself, so sometimes do I. And I do this with tears and with sorrow. It makes me sick."— *Sermon on " Future Punishment,"* p. 109.

In short, you confess yourself in almost total darkness respecting the spiritual world and all its grand realities. You say, in your sermon on "The Hereafter," which has induced me to address you at this time: —

"That great Future to which we are going is now all haze, with here and there a single point jutting out before us.

"To those, then, who ask what are to be the conditions in the other life of the countless myriads of men who have been going out of this world through countless ages, all the answer that can be given, is, We know not. We know not whether from other sources than this earth heaven is thronged and populated. We know not where heaven is. We know not what it is. It has not been revealed to us. There is not a word from the beginning of the Bible to the end, that can tell you definitely where heaven is, or what it is. (!) It is the place where the blessed are. *Place?* That term smacks of physical matter; and so far it is an imperfect term. Where the blessed are, is heaven; but whether it is near or far, whether it is above or below, we know not. We are not in a state to know. . . . You may say, 'Thus fondly have I thought; thus am I glad to believe;' but nothing more have you permission to say."

Again, in the same discourse:

"We know not whether there are to be national divisions, communal groups, or anything such as we have here. The mode of future being transcends anything that we know. We are as unable to understand it as a dog is to understand the nature of a commonwealth. Go, try to explain to the next intelligent creature below you all that you know of virtue, and disinterestedness, and love, and beauty. Explain a joke to a dog, if you can. Here are beings one or two ranks below you; and it is absolutely impossible to explain to a lower state of faculty the qualities of a higher state, or of a higher class of faculties superinduced upon a lower one. We stand in the line of the same analogy; and it is impossible to explain to us the evolvements which come from new faculties, or from old faculties developed to such a degree that they are to all intents and purposes new to us."

And again :

"I believe that we shall know our children [in the Hereafter], as they shall know us — not only as well as we know them, but far better. Will they not have grown? Very likely. I do not know. ‍ I cannot say."

"If you ask why God did not reveal more to us respecting the Hereafter, I reply by asking, Why do not you explain something of the domesticities of life to a dog? He could not understand it if you did. And we could not understand that which relates to the future [life] if God should explain it to us."

How do you know we could not? — permit me to ask. How do you know but our life beyond the grave, is merely a continuation of the present life of our spirits ? — a more complete unfolding of our souls' capabilities and essential characteristics or ruling loves ? — necessitating, therefore, civil, social, industrial, and domestic arrangements in the other world so nearly allied to those in this, that we could not only understand but greatly profit by them if they were revealed to us ? Do you not see that, without some change of your present mental attitude, you would inevitably deprive yourself, and others over whom you have influence, of the blessings of any revelation which God *might* be pleased to make concerning the Hereafter? You would render such a revelation, should it ever be made, altogether nugatory; for you would persuade yourself and others that it could not be from God, and therefore not true, because God would not attempt to explain what men are incapable of understanding.

Then do you really believe that the death of the body (which is the mere covering or husk of the spirit) works such a stupendous change in all our human characteristics — in our thoughts, dispositions, feelings, desires, motives and purposes — that we in the flesh are as incapable of understanding the condition (were it revealed) of those in the other world, as dogs are incapable "of understanding the nature of a commonwealth," or of appreciating the amenities or "domesticities" of our human life? Such seems to be your meaning. But how can you be so unreasonable and unphilosophical, not to say unscriptural? For the angel, you remember, said to John, when he was in the spirit, "I am thy fellow-servant, and of thy brethren the prophets." This, certainly, is an acknowledgment of close relationship — of similarity, yes, of absolute identity, as to species, nature and essence. A man would hardly address such language as this of the angel to a dog — would he?

And so, consistently enough with your confessed ignorance of nearly everything pertaining to the future life, you leave your ten thousand eager and inquiring readers to picture, each one for himself, such a condition of things in the Hereafter, as his own imagination may suggest. For you say that, in respect to "those things which a mother's heart, or a father's heart, or a lover's heart, or a friend's heart craves to know, there is no answer. But you are left to your own liberty. As a poet is left to imagine what he pleases, and as an artist is left to draw what he pleases, so you may imagine and draw what you please" concerning the life beyond the grave.

And, according to the teaching of your sermon from which I have here quoted, men are to remain forever in this impenetrable darkness concerning the spiritual realm? The inhabitants of this world will never know anything about that other world which they are here to prepare for, and in which they are to live forever! If I understand you, God will never (in your opinion) make any disclosures concerning that world, because, if He should, men could not understand them any more than a dog "can understand the nature of a commonwealth," or appreciate the sanctity of marriage.

Yet we are taught to pray that the Lord's will may be done on earth as it is done in heaven. Are we, then, never to know *how* his will is done in heaven? or how the angels live, and what is the chief source of their abounding joy? We are promised a time, too, when the Spirit of truth shall come, and shall guide men into all truth. Are you quite sure that "*all* truth" does not embrace *any* truth concerning the life after death, or concerning the condition of things in the Hereafter?—truth which such multitudes of human hearts long to know?

Moreover, a time is prophesied of, when "the glory

of the Lord shall be revealed"; when "the tabernacle of God shall be with men; . . and God himself shall be with them, their God"; when "the earth shall be full of the knowledge of the Lord, as the waters cover the sea"; when the Lord Jesus will come again to our human world, that is, to the understandings and hearts of men — breaking through the clouds of Scripture, or the obscuring mists of its literal sense — with an illuminating power scarce dreamed of hitherto; or, as the prophecy reads, "with power and great glory." When the dawn of that glorious Era begins, are you sure that none of the old darkness which has so long hung over the tomb will be dispersed, and no new and rejoicing light concerning the great Hereafter be diffused among men? Are you so sure of this that you would not look at or listen to any such alleged disclosure, however well authenticated might be its claim to a heavenly or even a divine origin? If so, then you may deprive yourself and others of a grand inheritance — nay, of the richest boon which it is in God's power to bestow upon the children of men.

Yet you say: "I know that we shall be as the angels of God; I know that we shall be satisfied, because we shall be like Him; I know that we shall be sons of God." What! — all of us? Shall we *all* be as the angels? — *all* be like God? — *all* be sons of God? — the righteous and the wicked? — the members of the Tammany and Erie "Rings," as well as the members of Plymouth church? This can hardly be your meaning. Yet there is nothing in your sermon to prevent your being so understood.

But to show that, after all, this declared knowledge about being "as the angels," "sons of God," etc., amounts to nothing, you immediately add: "Nobody can now tell what that means." Strange knowledge, that which leaves a man in utter ignorance of the meaning of what he says he knows. And then, of what conceivable use can such knowledge be? Suppose I am to be king some day, and I should say I *know* I shall be. But suppose I don't know the meaning of the expression; don't know whether to be king, means to be a pick-axe, a puppy, or a spirito-celestignifera; of what practical value would such knowledge be to me or any one else, I wonder? Would it stimulate me, or enlighten me, or help me in any way to prepare myself for the kingly office?

But already this letter has exceeded the limits I had prescribed. And yet I have scarcely reached the threshold of what I desire to say. I will only add here, that you are *entirely mistaken* in supposing that God has vouchsafed no revelation to men respecting their condition in the great Hereafter. He *has* made a very full revelation of the great facts and laws of the spiritual world, and of the condition of various classes of persons there. This, I think I may say, *I know*. And in a future communication I will tell you how I know it — and shall invite your special attention to the revelation itself, or to some of the things contained therein. Meanwhile I remain, with the highest esteem,

Your Friend and Brother,

B. F. BARRETT.

II.

SWEDENBORG'S CLAIM—AND CREDIBILITY.

My Dear Brother: — In my previous letter, I said you are mistaken in supposing that God has vouchsafed no revelation concerning the life beyond the grave; as you are, also, in thinking that if He should reveal the condition of things in the other world, it would be useless, because the revelation would be quite beyond men's power of comprehension; would be like our attempting "to explain something of the domesticities of life to a dog." I maintain, contrary to your assertion, that God *has* made a very full revelation concerning the Hereafter. He has lifted the veil, and made known to all who are willing to accept the revelation, the great facts and laws of the spiritual world, showing the condition and manner of life of the various classes of persons who go there — the evil as well as the good. Of this I am confident; and if you will allow me, I will give you some of the grounds and reasons for my confidence.

I shall assume, in the outset, that there is a spiritual world, and that you believe in its reality. Its existence has been maintained by the best minds and most advanced thinkers in every age and nation. "All nations that are in any degree cultivated," says Jung Stilling, "possess the fundamental idea of God, of a world of spirits, and of the immortality of the soul." Says the Chinese sage, Confucius, "How vast is the power of spirits! An ocean of invisible Intelligences surrounds us. They are everywhere above us, on the right hand and on the left." And Dr. Watts, speaking of the occasional appearance of spirits to men, says: "The multitude of narrations which we have heard of in all ages, of the apparitions of the spirits of persons departed from this life, can hardly be all delusion and falsehood." And nearly all the great masters in literature, both of ancient and modern times, especially the great poets — how fully do they recognize the existence and reality of a spiritual world! With what frequency and familiarity do they speak of invisible intelligences, who are always present, and interested in the affairs of our world! The great Greek and Roman epics are all aglow with this faith in a spiritual realm. In the Iliad and Æneid spiritual beings are introduced with as great freedom, and almost as much frequency, as mortals. And the same may be said of the works of Tasso and Ariosto, Dante and Goethe, Shakespeare and Milton, Wordsworth and Coleridge, Tennyson and Mrs. Browning, Lowell and Longfellow.

And throughout the Bible, often on every page, both good and bad spirits — angels and devils — are spoken of with the same freedom and familiarity as men. There is never expressed the shadow of a doubt about their reality, nor about their presence with men and their interest in human affairs. Their existence is always assumed as if it were a universally admitted truth; and no attempt is made to prove it.

True, we read of a certain heretical sect, who maintained that "there is neither angel nor spirit." And, consistently with this, the same sect also held "that there is no resurrection." But Christ rebuked them for their unbelief, telling them that Abraham, Isaac, and Jacob are still living — in the invisible world of spirits, of course. He assures them that, contrary to their idea, there is such a thing as the resurrection of the dead, and that these men have actually attained unto the resurrection. This is his brief and conclusive argument: "Now that the dead *are* raised [not *will be* raised at some far distant day] even Moses showed at the bush." And *how* did Moses show this at the bush? Why, by calling the Lord "the God of Abraham and the God of Isaac and the God of Jacob." But what evidence does this furnish that these men were still living, and had already attained unto the resurrection? Mark the conclusion of the Saviour's argument: "For He is not a God of the dead, but of the living; for *to Him* all are living." As if he had said: "These men, it is true, have passed beyond the material realm. Our natural senses can take no cognizance of them. To our dull perceptions they no longer live. To us they seem dead and gone. Not so, however, to Him whose eye penetrates all realms. *He* sees that these men (and all others who have disappeared from this sensuous sphere) are as truly alive now as they ever were. To Him, *all* human beings — whether in the flesh or out of the flesh — are alive; and as truly alive out of as in it. According to the teaching of Moses, whom ye profess to believe, He is still their God; and '*He* is not a God of the dead, but of the living.' His all-piercing eye sees them in that spiritual realm where they now are, as distinctly as it could in this realm of matter; and He knows, therefore, that they are still alive. 'To *Him*, all are living.'"

And not only does the Bible throughout assume the existence of angels and spirits, but it tells us, as you know, of their having been often seen by men. Witness the angelophanies recorded in the Old Testament — the appearance of angels to Abraham, Gideon, Manoah and others. Witness the appearance of Moses and Elias on the mount of transfiguration, hundreds of years after the death of their material bodies; the appearance to Mary, also, of "two angels in white, sitting, the one at the head and the other at the feet where the body of Jesus had lain;" and the myriads of angels whom the beloved disciple tells us he heard and saw when he was "in the spirit." And that these were all human beings, who had once been denizens of this natural world, is evident from the answer John received, when he asked who they were and whence they came: "These are they who came out of great tribulation, and have washed their robes, and made them white in the blood of the Lamb."

The existence, then, of a spiritual realm, inhabited by a countless multitude of spirits who were once clothed with material flesh, being admitted, is it not reasonable to expect that God would, some time or other, disclose to mortals here below some of the grand realities of that realm?—its scenery, and the laws which underlie and determine it?—the appearance of its inhabitants, their character, manner of life, social arrangements, varied activities, and the chief source of their joys—and sorrows, too, if they have any? To know how the angels live, or how the Lord's will is done in heaven—may not this be a means of helping us toward the attainment of the heavenly life? And may not an accurate account of the condition of the wicked and their manner of life in the Hereafter, exert a powerful influence on the character and conduct of men on earth?—especially if the intimate connection between the two worlds be clearly revealed, and the life yonder be shown to be but a continuation and fuller unfolding of the life begun and the character established here.

I put this interrogatively. But I am quite sure how you and every other sensible person will answer these questions. I am sure your answer will agree with the experience of the thousands who have already accepted the revelation which God has been pleased to make on this subject, and who know that they have been greatly enlightened, comforted and blessed thereby.

Then the gloomy doubts and fears of thousands and

tens of thousands in regard even to the soul's immortality, and the intense longing of millions of stricken hearts to know something positive and definite concerning that world to which their dearly loved ones have gone, added to some of your own sad confessions about the great Hereafter — may not these be accepted as among the sure prophecies that the darkness which has hitherto hung over the grave, will not always remain there?

But I affirm with much confidence that the veil *has been* lifted. The Lord has graciously revealed the grand realities of the spiritual world. And there is now no reason why any one should longer remain ignorant of the condition of things in the realm beyond the grave, unless he chooses to. Emanuel Swedenborg says:

"Hitherto it has been unknown, even to Christians, that there is a spiritual world inhabited by spirits and angels, distinct from the natural world inhabited by men. Lest, therefore, from ignorance of the existence of such a world, and the doubts respecting the reality of heaven and hell which result from such ignorance, men should be so infatuated as to become naturalists and atheists, it has pleased the Lord to open my spiritual sight, and, as to my spirit, to elevate me into heaven and let me down into hell, and to exhibit to my view the nature of both. It has thus been made evident to me that there are two worlds completely distinct from each other: one, called the spiritual world, all the objects of which are spiritual; the other, called the natural world, all the objects of which are natural; also that spirits and angels live in their world, and men in theirs; furthermore, that every man passes by death from his world into the other, wherein he lives forever." — *Intercourse between the Soul and the Body*, n. 3.

Again he says, in his treatise on Heaven and Hell, n. 1:

"The man of the church at this day knows scarcely anything about heaven or hell, nor yet about his own life after death, although these things are all treated of in the Word; nay, many even among those who were born within the church deny these things, saying in their hearts, Who has ever come thence and told us? Lest, therefore, such a negative principle, which rules especially among those who possess much worldly wisdom, should also infect and corrupt the simple in heart and faith, it has been granted me to associate with angels and to converse with them as one man with another, and also to see the things which are in the heavens as well as those which are in the hells; and this for the space of thirteen years, and so to describe these things from what I have myself seen and heard, — in the hope that ignorance may thus be enlightened and incredulity dissipated. The reason that such immediate revelation is made at this time, is, that this is what is meant by the coming of the Lord."

Again, in a letter to Rev. Dr. Hartley, he says:

"I have been called to a holy office by the Lord, who most graciously manifested himself in person to me his servant, in the year 1745, and then opened my sight into the spiritual world, and endowed me with the gift of conversing with spirits and angels, which has been continued to me to this day. From that time I began to print and publish various *arcana* which have been either seen by me or revealed to me; as concerning heaven and hell; the state of man after death; the true worship of God; the spiritual sense of the Word; and many other highly important matters tending to salvation and true wisdom."

Statements like the foregoing occur many times in the writings of the Swedish seer, and they are always made with equal clearness, simplicity, and positiveness. Now you, I presume, are familiar with the history and character of the man who sets up this extraordinary claim. Doubtless you have read his biography. And if so, you know that there never lived a person whose positive assertion was more worthy of credit than his. You know that he was a man of extensive and profound learning, of vast scientific attainments, and of the rarest sincerity, truthfulness and piety. You know that, in statements like those above cited, he is every whit as worthy to be believed as the apostle Paul or John. Professor Von Görres, of the University of Munich, says:

"Swedenborg was not a man to be carried away by an unbridled imagination, still less did he ever manifest during his whole life the slightest symptom of mental aberration. . . He was in life and disposition so blameless, that no man dare ever intimate any suspicion of concerted deception; and posterity have no right to call into question the unsuspected testimony of those who lived in the same age as Swedenborg, and who knew him well: if this mode of judgment be permitted, all historical evidence, even the holiest and most venerable, might be reduced to nothing."

And what is the testimony in regard to his character, furnished by his cotemporaries and acquaintance? Carl Robsam, director of the bank of Sweden, knew him intimately, and often visited him at his house. And he says:

"He loved truth and justice in all his feelings and actions. He was not only a learned man and a gentleman after the manner of the times, but a man so distinguished for wisdom as to be celebrated throughout Europe."

Count Andrew Van Hopken, the prime minister of Sweden, speaks of him in a letter to General Tuxen, as "a pattern of sincerity, of virtue, and of piety," and says:

"I have not only known him these two and forty years, but have also for some time daily frequented his company. And I do not recollect to have ever known a man of more uniformly virtuous character than Swedenborg; always contented, never fretful or morose, although throughout life his soul was occupied with sublime thoughts and speculations."

Dr. Messiter, an eminent physician of London, who

also knew him intimately, says, in a letter to one of the professors in the Glasgow University :

"I can with truth assert, that he is truly amiable in his morals, most learned and humble in his discourse, and superlatively affable, humane and courteous in his behavior; and this, joined with a solidity of understanding and penetration far above the level of an ordinary genius."

Rev. Dr. Hartley, himself a man of great sincerity and rare piety, was on terms of intimacy with him for many years; and this is his testimony:

"The great Swedenborg was a man of uncommon humility. He was of a catholic spirit, and loved all good men of every church, making at the same time all candid allowance for the innocence of involuntary error. . . . It may reasonably be supposed that I have weighed the character of our illustrious author in the scale of my best judgment, from the personal knowledge I had of him, from the best information I could procure respecting him, and from a diligent perusal of his writings; and according thereto I have found him to be the sound divine, the good man, the deep philosopher, the universal scholar, and the polite gentleman; and I further believe that he had a high degree of illumination from the Spirit of God, was commissioned by Him as an extraordinary messenger to the world, and had communication with angels and the spiritual world far beyond any since the time of the apostles."

Another cotemporary and intimate acquaintance says of him:

"He was of such a nature that he could impose on no one. He always spoke the truth in every little matter, and would not have made any evasion though his life had been at stake."

Such is the uniform testimony of the great seer's cotemporaries and acquaintance, to his exalted wisdom and learning, and his rare truthfulness, sincerity, humility and piety. No one who knew him, ever had any counter testimony to offer. And in perfect harmony with this, are the following "Rules of Life," which were found after his decease noted down in several of his manuscripts — evidently intended for private use, as we nowhere meet with them in his published works: —

1. "Often to read and meditate on the Word of the Lord.

2. "To submit everything to the will of Divine Providence.

3. "To observe in everything a propriety of behavior, and always to keep the conscience clear.

4. "To discharge with fidelity the functions of my employment and the duties of my office, and to render myself in all things useful to society."

Such was the character of the man, who has solemnly declared more than a hundred times that his spiritual senses were opened, and that he was thereby intromitted into the spiritual world, and permitted, for the space of nearly thirty years, to see and converse with angelic and infernal spirits, and so to learn all about the great Hereafter — or the condition of both the righteous and the wicked in the life beyond the grave.

Now if Paul's statement about his being caught up to the third heaven on a certain occasion, or his account of the wonderful experience he had on his way to Damascus, is to be accepted as altogether credible (and you, I presume, do not think of questioning his word, or his perfect sanity), I submit that Swedenborg's solemn and oft-repeated declaration about his intromission into the spiritual world, and his long and open intercourse with both angels and devils, is not a whit less credible. What good reason has any candid mind to offer for accepting the testimony of the great apostle, and ruling out that of the Swedish seer? Can you give any?

Suppose our own Washington, or Franklin, or any other distinguished and upright American citizen, had solemnly and repeatedly declared that, every day for the space of six years or more, he had, in a state of full wakefulness, seen and conversed with the spirits of several deceased friends, as men see and converse with each other. And suppose he had left a complete record of such experience; what should we say of it? Should we pronounce it incredible, because such alleged experience is unusual? Or should we say the man was deranged? — or that he was dreaming? I doubt if *you* would say either. If not, why, then, should Swedenborg's testimony respecting his own experience be rejected as incredible, or as evidencing some mental aberration?

But what, I hear you ask, has this alleged seer told us about the Hereafter? What has he revealed respecting the future life? Let us look at his alleged disclosures, and see whether they are worthy of the origin claimed for them. Perhaps the revelation itself will enable us to judge of the sanity or insanity — the credibility or incredibility — of the seer. Undoubtedly it will. And I shall, in a future communication, invite your candid attention to a few of the things concerning the other world, which, according to Swedenborg's declaration and my own belief, the Lord has graciously revealed through him. Meanwhile, I remain, as ever,

Your Friend and Brother,

B. F. BARRETT.

III.

HIS PHILOSOPHY OF SPIRIT-SEEING.

My Dear Brother: — In my last letter I told you what Swedenborg claims, or what he professes to have been divinely commissioned to reveal. He declares, as you saw from the passages quoted (and similar declarations are of frequent occurrence in his writings), that it had pleased the Lord to open his spiritual senses, and thus to intromit him into the spiritual world, and enable him to make a true revelation of the realities of that world; — to tell us, from his long and open intercourse with spirits and angels, what is the actual condition in the Hereafter of both the righteous and the wicked. Doubtless you will admit that the revelation he professes to make, or the information he pretends to give, is very desirable, and *may* be of great practical moment. But is it true? is the question. And how can we be satisfied, either of its truth or falsity? This is the inquiry which, I doubt not, suggests itself to your mind and that of every other thoughtful Christian. The inquiry is at once natural and pertinent. And while I hope to answer it satisfactorily before concluding this series of letters, I shall in the present epistle take but a single step in that direction.

If Swedenborg's pretended disclosures concerning the other world, or the condition of various classes of persons there, be not true, then he must have been a most villanous impostor, or must have labored under a strange hallucination; and this, too, for the space of nearly thirty years. But the testimony which all his cotemporaries and acquaintance bear to the rare simplicity, sincerity and truthfulness of his character, forbid the idea of anything like imposture. This, I am sure, must be the verdict of every candid mind that will read what his biographers have written. From the testimony cited in my last letter—summary as it was—you will admit, I think, that no man ever lived who was more deserving of entire credit in statements like those in question, than Swedenborg. I submit that the well-known character of the man, renders it impossible that he could have knowingly and intentionally deceived. Not James nor John nor Paul, nor any other of the apostles, was more honest or truthful than Swedenborg; nor his statements touching his own experience, or any facts that he may have observed, more worthy of credit.

But leaving his truthfulness or credibility quite out of the question, and looking entirely at the revelation itself, to what conclusion are we brought? Do we find here any evidence of imposture or delusion?—any traces of hallucination, or of a wild and wayward fancy? So far from it, I believe, and trust I shall be able to show, that the character of his disclosures proves the claim set up for them as a veritable revelation of the condition of things in the spiritual world, to be well-founded. And in this I find myself supported by the belief and testimony of thousands who have examined the revelation thoroughly enough to understand it; and among these are some of the clearest, strongest, acutest and most logical minds in Christendom. In his account of "things heard and seen" in the spiritual world, the Swedish seer has given us a pneumatology so grand, beautiful, rational and philosophical, and in such entire harmony with the teachings of Scripture, the known laws of the human soul, and our highest conceptions of the Divine wisdom and love as well as of the life beyond the grave, that it is impossible for an intelligent and candid mind not to accept it as true, so soon as he thoroughly understands it. In my next letter I shall adduce the bulk of the evidence I intend to offer going to authenticate his extraordinary claim.

At present I invite your attention merely to the *manner* of his intromission into the spiritual world, as explained by himself. He says it was through the opening of his spiritual senses that he was enabled to hold visible and audible communication with spirits, and to see and describe the things of their world. The spirit of man, according to his teaching, is a spiritual organism, composed of spiritual substance as the body is of material substance; and is in the human form. It has arms, hands, legs, feet, and all the other members that belong to the material body. It is also endowed with the senses of seeing, hearing, feeling, etc., far more acute and perfect, too, than the bodily senses. But these senses (for wise and excellent reasons which he explains) are ordinarily closed while the spirit tabernacles in the flesh; yet they may be, and often have been, opened in men while living in this material realm. And when opened, a person can see and hear spirits as plainly as we can see and hear each other; and can discern the objects of their world as clearly as we, with our natural eyes, can discern the objects of this.

This explains the philosophy of spirit-seeing, according to the teaching of the great Swede. Spirits are not seen with the same eyes as people and objects round about us in this world are seen; but with the eyes of the spirit which are usually closed, though they *may* be as suddenly and as quietly opened as our bodily eyes. In this way people in the natural world have frequently seen the spirits of their deceased friends in the spiritual world; not knowing, however, at the time, but they were seeing them with their natural eyes. This is the explanation of the angelophanies of which the Bible makes such frequent mention. It was in this way that the women saw the angels at the sepulchre of our Lord; that the Judean shepherds beheld that "multitude of the heavenly host," and heard their celestial anthem; that the disciples on the mount of transfiguration saw Moses and Elias, and the face of Jesus shining as the sun; that Paul, when on his way to Damascus, saw, as he tells us (and it was "at midday," observe), "a light from heaven above the brightness of the sun;" and that the seer of Patmos saw myriads of angels, and heard their hallelujahs.

Now I submit that this is the most rational and philosophical explanation of spirit-seeing that has ever been given. Since man is immortal, and we are assured by the great apostle that "there is a natural body and there is a spiritual body," and that this latter is what rises or comes into a state of full wakefulness when the former is laid aside, it is easy to believe that the spirit has senses which are opened when the body dies; and which *may be* opened and occasionally *are* opened in persons yet living in the flesh. This theory shows us, too, why it is that spirits, when seen, appear so suddenly, and as suddenly vanish. The opening of the spiritual eyes causes them to appear, and the shutting of these eyes causes them to vanish; just as natural objects reveal themselves to us as soon as our bodily eyes are opened, and disappear the instant these eyes are shut.

Then see how well Paul's remarkable experience agrees with what Swedenborg says about the light of the spiritual world, and the sun there; and how easy of explanation it is upon his theory of pneumatology. He says: "The light in heaven exceeds the noon-day light of this world in a degree surpassing all belief. The heavenly inhabitants, however, receive no light from this world, because they are above or within the sphere of that light [being in a purely spiritual realm]; but they receive light from the Lord, who is to them a sun." (*Arcana Cœlestia*, n. 1521.) Again he says: "The sun of heaven is the Lord; the light there is divine truth, and the heat is divine good [or love], both of which proceed from the Lord as a sun." (*Heaven and Hell*, n. 117.) And that sun being, as he says, immensely more brilliant than the sun of our world, we have only to suppose that Paul's spiritual eyes were suddenly opened even to the celestial degree, to understand how there could appear to him, "at mid-day, a light from heaven *above the brightness of the sun.*"

The same theory, too, furnishes us with an easy and philosophical explanation of the Saviour's appearance to Peter, James and John on the mount of transfiguration, when, as the record says, "his face did shine as the sun, and his raiment was white as the light;" also of his appearance to John in Patmos, when "his eyes were as a flame of fire; . . . and his countenance was as the sun shineth in his strength." And observe, this appearance is said to have occurred to the beloved disciple when he was "*in the spirit*" — language clearly indicating that the manifestation occurred in a realm within or above the natural.

And not only is Swedenborg's theory in regard to spirit-intercourse the only rational and philosophical one I have ever met with, but it is abundantly sustained by the Scripture record. The Bible clearly recognizes both the existence of spiritual senses in men, and the possibility of these senses being opened — yea, the fact that they have actually *been* opened. Take, for example, the case recorded in 2 Kings, 6th chapter. When "the servant of the man of God," having risen early in the morning, beheld the armed host which had been sent to Dothan to capture one poor prophet, he cried out, "Alas, my master! How shall we do?" And the prophet answered: "Fear not; for they that be with us are more than they that be with them. And Elisha prayed and said: Lord, I pray thee, open his eyes that he may see. And the Lord opened the eyes of the young man, and he saw; and behold, the mountain was full of horses and chariots of fire round about Elisha."

Now what kind of eyes did "the man of God" refer to in his prayer, and what kind of eyes do you think were opened in his servant on that occasion? Can there be any doubt that they were the eyes of his spirit? The agencies of Divine Providence which engirded. the prophet, and no doubt were visible to him, were at first unseen by his servant; and no wonder that the latter cried out as he did, when he beheld the Syrian host by which the town was beleaguered. But soon as his spiritual eyes were opened, he saw, in the inner realm of spirits, his master's strong defence, represented by the mountain "full of horses and chariots of fire round about Elisha;" for "all things seen in the spiritual world," says Swedenborg, "are representative and significative."

We see, then, that the explanation which the seer has

given us of the philosophy of spirit-seeing, and of the manner of his own intromission into the spiritual realm, is at once rational and Scriptural. It furnishes an easy explanation, also, of the angelophanies recorded in the Bible, and of the numerous and well-authenticated cases of the visible manifestation of spirits to men, which history records. And it is the only explanation I have ever met with, which fully satisfies the demands of reason.

A rational theory of pneumatology, I submit, is one of the great needs of the Christian churches of to-day. There is scarcely anything which they need so much. They need it to enable them to accept, and to know how to deal wisely with, the substantial facts of modern spiritualism. *You* need it yourself, my brother, more than almost anything else. It would add immensely to the power and effectiveness of your preaching, as well as to the satisfaction, joy and spiritual edification of your numerous hearers and readers. And such a theory, rely upon it, you will find fully unfolded in Swedenborg's treatise on Heaven and Hell — a work which should be carefully read and studied by every Christian minister. The part on Heaven contains more than forty chapters, of which the following are some of the headings:

"The Divine of the Lord makes heaven." "The Divine of the Lord in heaven is love to him and charity toward the neighbor." "Heaven consists of innumerable societies." "Every society in heaven resembles one man." "The sun in heaven." "Light and heat in heaven." "The garments with which the angels appear clothed." "The habitations and mansions of the angels." "Divine worship in heaven." "The speech of the angels." "Writings in heaven." "The wisdom of the angels." "The state of peace in heaven." "Heaven and hell are from the human race." "The rich and poor in heaven." "Gentiles [people outside of Christendom] in heaven." "Infants in heaven." "Employments of the angels." "Heavenly joy and happiness."

Now if you will read attentively any one of these chapters, and bring all the best powers of your understanding and the finest intuitions of your heart, together with all known truth and your highest conceptions of the wisdom and love of God, to bear upon it, you will, I think, be constrained to say, "Verily, that must be so. I see here not one of the signs of fanaticism or delusion. Every sentence bears the impress of truth and soberness. All that is here related, accords with reason and Scripture and the known laws of the human soul, as well as with my highest conception of the character of God, and of his ultimate design in the creation of man. It is but the normal and beautiful blossoming forth of regenerate souls when released from their earthly wrappages."

And as you read, please remember that Swedenborg is not here giving us his own fancies or speculations, or the conclusions of his understanding merely; but is telling us (and you will admit that a more truthful man than he never lived) of "things *heard and seen*," and in *this* manner learned, when his spiritual senses were opened. And what he relates on several of these subjects — though very different from the popular belief at the time he lived and wrote — is so reasonable in itself, that it is generally accepted by the best minds in nearly all the churches of to-day; though scarcely one in fifty, perhaps, is aware that the truth he accepts on these subjects, and which seems so obvious in the light of the present day, was unknown and unrecognized until revealed through Swedenborg.

But the question, after all, whether we have a true and divinely authorized revelation of the Hereafter — that is, of the state of life beyond the grave — can best be answered by the revelation itself. I shall, therefore, in my next letter, invite your candid attention to some of the things contained in this alleged revelation; and shall leave you to judge whether, in view of their intrinsic reasonableness and important practical bearings, the revelation itself is to be regarded as spurious or genuine. Meanwhile, I remain

Truly and Affectionately your Brother,

B. F. BARRETT.

IV.

VINDICATION OF HIS CLAIM.

My Dear Brother: — Let me advise you at once, that the present letter will be a long one — longer, probably, than you will care to read at one sitting. But you will not, I trust, be deterred by its length from giving it a patient and careful perusal. I think it will interest, and hope it may profit you; as I shall herein spread before you a considerable amount of evidence (not a tithe, however, of what might be offered), in vindication of Swedenborg's extraordinary claim; — evidence of the best kind, too, because drawn from the disclosures themselves which he claims to have been divinely authorized to make.

You know the nature and extent of his claim — from my previous letters, if not from a perusal of the seer's own writings. You know he professed to have been so illumined by the Holy Spirit, as to be able to understand and explain the spiritual meaning of God's Word; and to have had his spiritual senses opened for the space of nearly thirty years, whereby he was enabled to hold visible and audible communication with the denizens of the other world during that long period. And you know what kind of a man he was. You know he was incapable of deliberate falsehood. No candid mind ever did or ever will harbor the suspicion of anything like wilful imposture in his case.

But he *may* have been self-deceived — honestly so. He may have innocently labored under a strange hallucination. He may have thought that he saw people and objects in the spiritual world — that he saw and conversed with angels and devils — when in reality it was but the effect of his own imagination. This, no doubt, is the opinion of many honest people at the present day, who are not familiar with his writings. Possibly your own mind may rest in this conclusion.

And what is the best way to settle the question? How are we to know whether his alleged disclosures concerning the other world, be facts or fancies? — whether they be a veritable and divinely authorized revelation, or the ingenious coinings of the man's own brain — the products of a vivid but wild and wayward imagination? I answer: By a careful examination of the revelation itself; surveying it in the light of Scripture, reason, historical facts, human experience and the known laws of the human soul. Is not this the fair and the *only* fair way of reaching a just conclusion in the case?

If a man should come and say to you: "Mr. Beecher, I have discovered a mine of gold on the south-west corner of your farm;" you might be excused, perhaps, for doubting his word, even though his reputation for truthfulness were well established. But if he should offer to take you to the spot, dig up the sand and sift out the grains before your eyes; quarry the rocks and show you the nuggets; and, that you might know that it was pure gold and nothing else, should invite you to take some specimens to the laboratory, and there subject them to the recognized chemical tests; and if, instead of accepting his invitation, you should turn away with a shrug, saying, "Impossible! Nothing of the sort has ever been told me before. There can't be any gold on my farm. It is all in your eye. The mere offspring of a lively imagination;" would you be acting wisely or reasonably? I think not.

Let me ask you, then, my dear brother, to examine carefully the extracts I shall here lay before you; to subject them to all the known tests of rational and spiritual truth; and then say whether they look like the speculations of an innocent dreamer and the utterances of a fanatic, or—what they boldly claim to be — a veritable revelation from God out of heaven concerning the life beyond the grave. And bear in mind that these extracts are taken from the work entitled, "Heaven and its Wonders; and Hell. From *things heard and seen.*"

DEATH AND RESURRECTION.

Hear, first, what the seer has to say about the nature of the resurrection. You know what doctrine was held on this subject at the time he lived and wrote. It was, that the bodies we now have—our *material* bodies which are laid off at death—are one day to be raised to life again, and reunited to our souls. This was what Christians understood by the resurrection. Many religious teachers still hold this doctrine. But *you* do not. For in your sermon on "The Hereafter" you say:

"There is to be a body raised; but it is not to be a physical body. It is to be a spiritual body." And in another of your printed discourses, I find the following:

"We are not going to carry this body into the other life. There has been a vast amount of speculation and misapprehension upon this subject, it seems to me. . . . We are to have bodies in heaven, but not these bodies. If there can be anything definitely stated in the Latin, or in the Greek, or in any other language, it seems to me that this declaration of the Apostle is a positive statement: 'Flesh and blood shall not inherit the kingdom of God.' Now to tell me that we shall have these bodies, but that they shall have no flesh and blood, is to play upon words."

And you will find among the more advanced religious thinkers of to-day, many to agree with you in this—although it is not, as you are well aware, the recognized orthodox doctrine of the resurrection. Thus the Rev. Mr. Sears, in his beautiful "Foregleams of Immortality," says:

"The artificial theologies do not make the resurrection

of man a fact included under the operation of any law whatsoever, but a monstrosity thrust in among the orderly operations of the Deity. They make it not only a miracle, but a miracle wrought mechanically, and not spiritually. The idea of God coming down to the cemeteries, and, potter-like, building up from their contents a set of human frames externally, and putting spirits into them afterward, is shocking enough, if we had not long ceased to be shocked by the fantasies of religious naturalism."— p. 80.

Again, in the same work: —

" The natural body is not the man, nor any essential part of him. The spirit itself is an immortal organism, folded in by its clay coverings in order, for probationary purposes, to hold connection awhile with material things. It is the most real part of man, since nearer in degree and kindred to the eternal realities. The resurrection is the emergence of the immortal being in a spiritual body out of material conditions, when first it has open relations with a spiritual world, and is set face to face with spiritual things."— p. 174

Now this (which seems to be your own idea) is precisely the doctrine promulgated by Swedenborg more than a hundred years ago; for he wrote:

"The spirit of man, after the dissolution of the body, is a man in all respects, except that he is not encompassed with the gross body which he had in the world. This he leaves when he dies, *nor does he ever resume it.* This continuation of life [or awakening to consciousness in the spiritual world] is meant by the resurrection." (N. J. D. 225-6.) When the body dies, "the man is said to die; but still the man does *not* die, but is only separated from the corporeal part which was of use to him in the world; for the man himself lives." — *Heaven and Hell*, n. 445.

And in perfect agreement with this, is the following which he relates from his own personal observation:

"The interiors belonging to my spirit have been opened by the Lord, and thus I have been permitted to converse with all whom I have ever known in the life of the body, — after their decease; with some for days, with some for months, and with some for a year; and with others also, — so many that I should not exaggerate were I to say a hundred thousand, — of whom many were in the heavens and many in the hells. I have also conversed with some two days after their decease, and have told them that preparations were now being made for their interment. They replied, that their friends did well to reject that which had served them for a body and its uses in the world; and they wished me to say, that they were not dead but alive, being men now just the same as before; that they had only migrated from one world to another; that they were not conscious of having lost anything, since they were in a body and in the possession of bodily senses as before, and in the enjoyment of understanding and will as before; and that they had thoughts, affections, sensations, and desires, similar to those which they had in the world.

"Most of those recently deceased, when they saw that they were still alive and men as before, and in a similar state, (for after death every one's state of life is at first such as it had been in the world, but that is gradually changed either into heaven or into hell,) were affected with new joy at being alive, and declared that they had not believed this. But they wondered very much that they should have lived in such ignorance and blindness concerning the state of their life after death; and especially that the man of the church should be in such ignorance and blindness." — H. H. 312.

FORM OF THE SPIRIT.

You know that the prevailing idea among Christians in Swedenborg's time was, that the soul or spirit of man was a subtle essence, an ethereal vapor, a thinking principle without organization, substance, or form of any kind. But can you conceive of a being capable of faith, hope, and charity, — capable of thinking, reasoning, rejoicing, and loving, without some kind of an organized form? Or can you conceive of a being endowed with *human capacities* without possessing the *human form?* I cannot.

The following is Swedenborg's testimony on this subject — very different, you observe, from the current belief of his day:

"That the spirit of man after its separation from the body is itself a man, and similar in form, has been proved to me by the daily experience of many years; for I have seen, heard, and conversed with spirits thousands of times, and have even talked with them on the prevailing disbelief that spirits are men; and have told them that the learned regard those as simple who think so. The spirits were grieved at heart that such ignorance still continues in the world, and especially within the church. But they remarked that this infidelity had emanated chiefly from the learned, who have thought of the soul from their corporeal-sensual apprehensions, and thence have concluded that it is mere thought, which, when viewed without any subject in and from which it exists, is like a volatile breath of pure ether, which cannot but be dissipated when the body dies. This is the foundation of the prevailing doctrine of the resurrection, and of the belief that the soul and body will be again united at the time of the last judgment."

"It is worthy of remark that the human form of every man after death is the more beautiful, the more interiorly he had loved divine truths and had lived according to them; for the interiors of every one are opened and formed according to his love and life; wherefore the more interior is the affection, the more conformable it is to heaven, and hence the more beautiful is the face. Therefore the angels of the inmost heaven are the most beautiful, because they are forms of celestial love." — Ibid. 456-9.

MAN ESSENTIALLY A SPIRIT.

And if the soul is in the human form, and is capable of thinking, reasoning and loving, after its separation from the body, what is more reasonable than to believe that it is an exquisite spiritual organism, endowed with the senses of seeing, hearing, feeling, etc., and these very acute and perfect? Accordingly Swedenborg says:

"The soul of man, about the immortality of which so many have written, is his spirit; for this is immortal as to all that pertains to it. It is this which thinks in the body, for it is spiritual; and what is spiritual lives spiritually, which is to think and will.

"Since everything that lives in the body, and from life acts and feels, belongs exclusively to the spirit, and nothing of it to the body, it follows that the spirit is the real man; or, what is the same, that man considered in himself is a spirit, and that the spirit is also in a form similar to that of the body; for whatever lives and feels in man belongs to his spirit — and everything in him, from his head to the sole of his foot, lives and feels.

"Man cannot see without an organ which is the subject of his sight; nor hear without an organ which is the subject of his hearing. Sight and hearing are nothing without these, nor can they exist. It is the same also with thought, which is internal sight; and with perception, which is internal hearing. Unless these existed in and from substances which are organic forms that are the subjects of those faculties, they could not exist at all.

"From these considerations it is manifest that the spirit of man is in a form as well as his body; and that its form is the human; and that it enjoys sensories and senses when separated from the body, the same as when it was in it; and that all the life of the eye and ear, in a word, all the sensitive life that man enjoys, belongs not to his body but to his spirit; for his spirit dwells in them and in every minutest part thereof. Hence it is that spirits see, hear and feel, the same as men; but after separation from the body, not in the natural but in the spiritual world."— Ibid. 432-434.

THE SUN OF HEAVEN.

If the spiritual world is a real world, we might reasonably expect there would be a sun there; and that the sun, like all else belonging to that world, would be spiritual in its nature. Such expectation, moreover, seems justified — does it not? — by the experience of the apostle Paul, the seer of Patmos, and the disciples on the mount of transfiguration. So Swedenborg, speaking from his personal observation and experience, says:

"The sun of the world does not appear in heaven, nor anything which exists from that sun. Yet there is a sun there, and light, and heat, and all things which are in the world, and a great many more, but not from a similar origin; for the things which exist in heaven are spiritual, and those which exist in the world are natural. The sun of heaven is the Lord. The light there is divine truth, and the heat is divine good, both of which proceed from the Lord as a sun. From that origin are all things which exist and appear in heaven. The Lord appears in heaven as a sun, because He is the divine love from which all spiritual things exist, as all natural things exist by means of the sun of this world. It is that love which shines as a sun.

"That the Lord actually appears in heaven as a sun, has not only been told me by the angels, but has also been given me occasionally to see."— Ibid. 117, 118.

And in his *Arcana Cœlestia*, he speaks of the intense brightness of this sun, as follows:

"The light in heaven is such as to exceed the noon-day light of this world in a degree surpassing all belief. The heavenly inhabitants, however, receive no light from the world, because they are above or within the sphere of that light; but they receive light from the Lord who is their sun." n. 1521.

LIGHT AND HEAT IN HEAVEN.

Both reason and Scripture, too, warrant the conclusion that there must be light and heat in the spiritual world. And these, like the sun from which they emanate, should be spiritual, should they not? This, at least, is the rational conclusion. But what says the Swedish seer about it? Hear him:

"That there is light in heaven cannot be comprehended by those who think only from nature; when yet the light there is so great, as to exceed by many degrees the mid-day light of the world. I have often seen it, even in the evening and night. At first I wondered when I heard the angels say, that the light of the world is little more than shade in comparison with the light of heaven; but since I have seen it, I can testify that it is so. Its whiteness and brilliancy surpass all description. The things seen by me in heaven, were seen in that light; thus more clearly and distinctly than things in the world.

"The light of heaven is not natural like that of the world, but spiritual; for it proceeds from the Lord as a sun. That which proceeds from the Lord as a sun, is called in heaven divine truth, although in its essence it is divine good united to divine truth. Hence the angels have light and heat; light from the divine truth, and heat from the divine good. From this consideration it is evident that the light and heat of heaven are not natural but spiritual from their origin.

"Divine truth is light to the angels, because they are spiritual and not natural. Spiritual beings see from their sun, and natural beings from theirs. Divine truth is the source whence the angels have understanding, and understanding is their internal sight which flows into and produces their external sight. Hence the things which appear in heaven from the Lord as a sun, appear in light. Such being the origin of light in heaven, therefore it varies according to the reception of divine truth from the Lord; or — what is the same — according to the intelligence and wisdom of the angels. It is therefore different in the celestial kingdom from what it is in the spiritual, and different in each society.

"Something shall now be said concerning the heat of heaven.— The heat of heaven in its essence is love. It proceeds from the Lord as a sun: and that this is the divine love in the Lord and from Him, has been shown in the preceding chapter. Hence it is evident that the heat of heaven is spiritual as well as its light; for it is from the same origin. There are two things which proceed from the Lord as a sun, divine truth and divine good. Divine truth in the heavens is light, and divine good is heat; but divine truth and divine good are so united, that they are not two, but one.

"The heat of heaven, like its light, is everywhere various. That in the celestial kingdom differs from that in the spiritual; and it differs also in every society. And not only does it differ in degree, but even in kind. It is more intense and pure in the Lord's celestial kingdom, because the angels there are more receptive of the divine good; it is less intense and pure in the Lord's spiritual kingdom, because the angels there are more receptive of divine truth; and it differs also in every society according to reception.

"There is heat also in the hells, but it is unclean. The heat in heaven is what is meant by sacred and celestial fire, and the heat of hell is what is meant by profane and infernal fire; and by both is meant love. Celestial fire means love to the Lord and love toward the neighbor, and every affection derived from these loves; and infernal fire means the love of self and the love of the world, and every lust derived from these loves." — Ibid. 127-134.

OBJECTS SEEN IN HEAVEN.

As spirits have eyes we should expect there would be a variety of objects in their world to look upon. The gift of such a sense or faculty as seeing, presupposes the existence of objects to be seen. Besides, a world in which there are no objects to be seen, would be — not a very desirable world for any one to live in. Deliver me, you would say, from a world that has nothing in it — or nothing to be seen. But according to Swedenborg there is a greater variety of objects in the spiritual than in the natural world. He says:

"The nature of the objects which appear to the angels in heaven, cannot be described in a few words. For the most part they are like the things on earth, but in form more perfect, and in number more abundant.

"The things which are in heaven cannot be seen with the bodily eyes, but with the eyes of the spirit; and these are opened when it pleases the Lord; and then man is withdrawn from the natural light in which he is by reason of the bodily senses, and is elevated into spiritual light in which he is by reason of his spirit. In that light I have seen the things which exist in heaven.

"But although the objects which appear in heaven are,

for the most part, similar to those which exist on earth, still they are not similar as to essence; for the things which are in heaven exist from the sun of heaven, and those which are on the earth, from the sun of the world. The things which exist from the sun of heaven are called spiritual, but those which exist from the sun of the world are called natural.

"The things which exist in heaven do not exist in the same manner as those which exist on earth. All things in heaven exist from the Lord according to their correspondence with the interiors of the angels; for the angels have both interiors and exteriors. The things which are in their interiors all have relation to love and faith, thus to will and understanding, — for will and understanding are their receptacles.

"Since all things which correspond to the interiors also represent them, therefore they are called REPRESENTATIVES; and since they vary according to the state of the interiors with the angels, therefore they are called APPEARANCES; — although the objects which appear before the eyes of angels in heaven, and which are perceived by their senses, appear and are perceived as much to the life as those on earth appear to man; yea, much more clearly, distinctly, and perceptibly. The appearances thence existing in the heavens, are called *real appearances*, because they really exist.

"To those who are in intelligence, there appear gardens and paradises full of trees and flowers of every kind,

The trees are planted in the most beautiful order, and so interwoven as to form arbors, with entrances of verdant fret-work, and walks around them,— all of such beauty as no language can describe. They who are distinguished for intelligence also walk there, and gather flowers. There are also species of trees and flowers there, such as were never seen and could not exist in the world. On the trees are fruits, according to the good of love in which the intelligent are principled. Such things are seen by them, because a garden and paradise, and also fruit-trees and flowers, correspond to intelligence and wisdom." — Ibid. 171-176.

THE ESSENCE OF HEAVEN.

The following is from the chapter, "The Divine of the Lord makes Heaven." It needs no explanation nor comment, and 1 shall therefore offer none.

"The angels taken collectively are called heaven, because they constitute it. Nevertheless it is the Divine proceeding from the Lord, which flows-in with the angels, and is received by them, which makes heaven in general and in particular. The Divine proceeding from the Lord is the good of love and the truth of faith. As far, therefore, as they receive good and truth from the Lord, they are angels, and are a heaven.

"Every one in heaven knows and believes, yea, perceives that he wills and does nothing of good from himself, and that he thinks and believes nothing of truth from himself, but from the Divine, thus from the Lord; and that the good and truth which are from himself, are not good and truth, because there is not in them life from the Divine. The angels of the inmost heaven also clearly perceive, and are sensible of, the influx; and so far as they receive it, they seem to themselves to be in heaven, because they are so far in love and faith, and so far in the light of intelligence and wisdom, and thence in heavenly joy. Since these things all proceed from the Divine of the Lord, and the angels possess heaven in them, it is evident that the Divine of the Lord makes heaven, and not the angels by virtue of anything properly their own. Hence it is that heaven in the Word is called the habitation of the Lord, and His throne; and that the dwellers there are said to be in the Lord.

"The angels, by virtue of their wisdom, go still further. They say that not only are all good and truth from the Lord, but also all of life. That all of life is from Him they also confirm by this consideration: that all things in the universe have reference to good and truth,—the life of man's will, which is the life of his love, to good, and the life of his understanding, which is the life of his faith, to truth. Therefore, since everything good and true comes from above, it follows that all of life also comes from thence. Because the angels believe this, therefore they refuse all thanks on account of the good they do; and are displeased and withdraw themselves if any one attributes good to them. They wonder how any one can believe that he is wise from himself, and that he does good from himself. Good done for the sake of one's self, they do not call good, because it is done from self; but good done for the sake of good, this they call good from the Divine; and they say that this good is what makes heaven.

"The Divine in heaven which makes heaven, is love; because love is spiritual conjunction. Love conjoins the angels with the Lord and with each other; and it conjoins them in such a manner, that they are all as one in the Lord's sight.

"There are two distinct loves in heaven, love to the Lord and love toward the neighbor. In the inmost or third heaven is love to the Lord; in the second or middle heaven, love toward the neighbor. Each proceeds from the Lord, and each makes heaven. How these two loves are distinguished, and how they are conjoined, appears very clearly in heaven, but only obscurely in the world. In heaven, to love the Lord does not mean to love Him as to his person, but to love the good which is from Him; and to love good, is to will and do good from love. And to love the neighbor does not mean to love a fellow-being as to his person, but to love the truth which is from the Word; and to love truth is to will and do it."—Ibid. 7, 8, 9, 14, 15.

MANY SOCIETIES IN HEAVEN.

All good people in this world, you know, are not exactly alike. Their goodness differs both in kind and degree. They are not all quite congenial; therefore, if left to act in freedom according to their internal promptings, they would not all seek each other's society. Only those who are in a similar kind and degree of good, are perfectly congenial and love to be together. Therefore, if each one takes his own character with him into the other world, we should expect as great a diversity among the angels in heaven, as we find among good people here on earth. And as a consequence of this, we should expect there would be innumerable societies in heaven, each composed of kindred souls drawn together and held together by mutual affinity; for only those who are in similar kinds and degrees of good, love to be together. And agreeably to this, Swedenborg says:

"The angels do not all dwell together in one place, but are distinguished into larger and smaller societies, according to the differences of the good of love and faith in which they are. They who are in similar good form one society. Goods in the heavens are of infinite variety; and every angel is such, in character, as is his own good.

"The angelic societies in the heavens are also distant from each other according to the general and specific differences of their goods; for distances in the spiritual world are from no other origin than from a difference in the state of the interiors; consequently, in the heavens, from a difference in the states of love. Those are far apart who differ much, and those are near who differ little. Similarity brings them together.

"Those of like character are brought together as it were spontaneously; for with their like, they are as with their own [relations], and at home; but with others, as with strangers and abroad. When they are with their like, they are also in their freedom, and thence in every delight of life. Hence it is evident that good consociates all in the heavens, and that all are distinguished according to its quality.

"All who are in similar good also know each other — although they had never met before — just as men in the world know their kindred, relations and friends; the reason is, that in the other life there are no kindreds, relationships, and friendships but such as are spiritual, that is, of love and faith. I have several times been permitted to see this, when I have been in the spirit, withdrawn as it were from the body, and thus in company with angels. On such occasions I have seen some who seemed as if I had known them from infancy; but others seemed wholly unknown to me. They who seemed as if known from infancy, were those who were in a state similar to the state of my spirit; but they who were unknown, were in a dissimilar state.

"All who belong to the same angelic society resemble each other in general, but not in particular. In heaven, all the interior affections appear and shine forth from the face,—for the face there is the external and representative form of these affections. No one in heaven is permitted to have a face that is not in correspondence with his affections. Hence also it is, that an angel who excels in wisdom, instantly discerns the character of another from his face."—Ibid. 41–48.

HEAVEN AND THE CHURCH WITHIN THE SOUL.

The prevailing idea in Swedenborg's day concerning heaven was, that it is a place into which people may be admitted by an act of immediate mercy — as a person from favor may be admitted into the palace of a prince. Contrary to this idea, he tells us that it is not a *place* but a *state of life;* that the essence of heaven is within the soul; and that, if any one should be elevated among the angels before the angelic state of life has been developed within him by his own voluntary effort, he would find no heaven there. On the contrary he would be unspeakably miserable, and would desire to depart from the society of those whose sphere was so uncongenial. None, he assures us, can really go to heaven and be happy there, save those who have something of heaven within themselves. And does not this agree with the teaching of the Lord himself? "The kingdom of God," He says, "cometh not with observation: Neither shall they say, Lo here! or, lo there! For, behold, the kingdom of

God is within you." Listen, now, to Swedenborg on this subject:

"It can in no case be said that heaven is without one, but that it is within him; for every angel receives the heaven which is without him according to the heaven which is within him. This plainly shows how much he is deceived, who believes that to go to heaven is merely to be elevated among the angels without regard to the quality of one's interior life; thus that heaven may be given to every one from immediate mercy; when yet, unless heaven be within a person, nothing of the heaven which is without him flows-in and is received. Many spirits entertain this opinion; and because of their belief they have been taken up into heaven. But when they came there, because their interior life was contrary to that of the angels, they were so blinded as to their intellectual faculties that they became like idiots, and were so tortured as to their will faculties that they behaved like madmen. In a word, they who go to heaven after living wicked lives, gasp there for breath, and writhe about like fishes taken from the water into the air, and like animals in the ether of an air-pump after the air has been exhausted. Hence it is evident that heaven is not without one, but within him.

"Heaven also exists wherever the Lord is acknowledged, believed in and loved. Variety in the worship of Him, arising from the variety of good in different societies, is not injurious, but advantageous; for the perfection of heaven results from such variety. . . . When a whole is composed of various parts, and these are arranged in a perfect form wherein each part joins itself to another as a sympathizing friend in the series, then it is complete. Now heaven is a whole composed of various parts arranged in the most perfect form; for the heavenly form is the most perfect of all forms. That all perfection results from this harmonious arrangement of parts that are different, is evident from all the beauty, pleasantness and delight which affect both the senses and the mind.

"The same may be said of the church as of heaven; for the church is the Lord's heaven upon earth. There are also many churches; and yet each one is called a church, and likewise is a church, so far as the good of love and faith rules therein. There also the Lord makes a whole from different parts, thus from several churches makes one church. The same, too, may be said of each member of the church in particular, as of the church in general; namely, that the church is within him and not without him; and that every man in whom the Lord is present in the good of love and faith, is a church. The same may also be said of a man in whom the church is, as of an angel in whom heaven is, that he is a church in the least form, as an angel is a heaven in the least form; and further, that a man in whom the church is, is a heaven equally with an angel; for man was created that he might go to heaven and become an angel; wherefore he who receives good from the Lord, is a man-angel." — Ibid. 54–57.

THE WHOLE HEAVEN RESEMBLES A MAN.

Among all of Swedenborg's alleged disclosures respecting the other world, there are few, perhaps, which, on their first announcement, are commonly regarded as more fanciful, or more indicative of mental disorder on the part of the seer, than what we find in the following paragraphs:

"That heaven in its whole complex resembles one man, is an arcanum not yet known in the world; but in the heavens it is very well known. The angels know that all the heavens, together with their societies, resemble one man; therefore also they call heaven THE GREATEST and THE DIVINE MAN; Divine from this, that the Divine of the Lord makes heaven.

"The angels, indeed, do not see heaven in the whole complex in the form of a man; for the whole heaven does not fall under the view of any angel. But they sometimes see remote societies, consisting of many thousands of angels, as one in such a form; and from a society as from a part, they form a conclusion concerning the whole, which is heaven. For in the most perfect form, the whole is as the parts, and the parts as the whole; the only difference being like that between similar things of greater and less magnitude.

"The reason why so many different things in man act as one, is, that there is nothing whatever in him which does not contribute something to the common weal, and perform some use. The whole performs use to its parts, and the parts perform use to the whole; for the whole is made up of the parts, and the parts constitute the whole; therefore they provide for each other, have respect to each other, and are conjoined in such a form that all and each have reference to the whole and its good. Hence it is that they act as one.

"The associations in the heavens are similar. They are joined together there according to their uses in a like form. Therefore they who do not perform use to the community, are cast out of heaven as things foreign to its nature. To perform use, is to desire the welfare of others for the sake of the common good; and not to perform use, is to desire the welfare of others, not for the sake of the common good, but for the sake of self. These latter love themselves supremely, but the former love the Lord above all things. Hence it is that they who are in heaven act in unison, not from themselves but from the Lord; for they regard Him as the one only Source of all things, and his kingdom as the community whose good is to be sought. This is meant by the Lord's words, 'Seek ye first the kingdom of God, and His righteousness, and all these things shall be added unto you.' Matt. vi. 33.

"They who, in the world, love the good of their country more than their own, and the good of their neighbor as their own, are they who, in the other life, love and seek the kingdom of the Lord, — for there the kingdom of the Lord is in the place of their country;

and they who love to do good to others, not for their own sake, but for the sake of the good, love their neighbor, — for in the other life good is the neighbor. All who are of this character are in the GRAND MAN; that is, in heaven." — Ibid. 59–65.

I am aware how absurd it must seem on its first announcement, to liken the whole heaven of angels to one man; or to call it, as Swedenborg often does, *Maximus Homo* — "the Grand Man." Yet it needs but little reflection to see that there is no other conceivable way in which the exact truth could be so well or so concisely expressed. For what is to be understood by the expression? Simply this: That the diversity, unity, harmony, mutual dependence and perfect concert of action existing among the societies which constitute the entire angelic heaven, are precisely similar to and correspondent with what exist among the various members and organs of the human body. The body consists of a great number of parts. And how diverse are these parts in form and function! Yet what entire agreement among them, notwithstanding this diversity! What beautiful, fraternal union! What harmonious and perfect concert of action! What utter dependence of each upon all the rest! If you desired something whereby to illustrate the most perfect unity and harmony, coupled with mutual dependence and the greatest conceivable variety, is not the human body the very thing you would select?

And when this idea of heaven comes to be generally

accepted by Christians, they will see that unity with diversity is agreeable to divine order; and that the numerous societies and churches on earth, however they differ in doctrine and ritual, may — and if animated by a heavenly spirit, will — nevertheless, live together and labor together, like the different members and organs of the human body, in perfect unity. You, my brother, can certainly understand and appreciate this new idea of heaven; and can readily see its practical bearings upon the church here below.

CHANGES OF STATE IN HEAVEN.

Variety and change everywhere mark the universe of God. How doleful would seem a world in which there is no change! Picture to yourself the most enchanting scene imaginable, the most delightful season of the year and time of day; and then imagine that scene and season and hour to be invariably the same! How soon you would tire of it! Before the lapse of three months — perhaps of one — you would long to have that scene changed, even though the change should be to something less lovely. And does not this prove that change, or the desire for it, is stamped on the soul itself? And if so, must not changes of state, involving corresponding changes in the outward or phenomenal world, be one of the conditions of happiness in the Hereafter? The following are among our seer's disclosures on this subject:

"States are predicated of life, and of those things which belong to life; and since angelic life is the life of love and faith, and thence of wisdom and intelligence, therefore states are predicated of these, and are called states of love and faith, and states of wisdom and intelligence.

"The angels are not constantly in the same state as to love, nor, consequently, as to wisdom; for all their wisdom is from love and according to it. Sometimes they are in a state of intense love, and sometimes in a state of love not so intense. It decreases by degrees from its greatest to its least. When they are in the greatest degree of love, they are in the light and heat of their life, or in their bright and delightful state; but when they are in the least degree, they are in shade and cold, or in their state of obscurity and undelight. From the last state they return again to the first; and so on.

"These states do not succeed each other uniformly, but with variety, like the variations of the state of light and shade, and of heat and cold; or like morning, noon, evening, and night, every day in the world, with perpetual variety throughout the year. They also correspond,— morning to a state of their love in brightness; noon to a state of their wisdom in brightness; evening to a state of their wisdom in obscurity; and night to a state of no love and wisdom. But it is to be observed that there is no correspondence of night with the states of life of those who are in heaven; but there is a correspondence of the twilight which precedes the morning. The correspondence of night is with those who are in hell. From this correspondence days and years in the Word signify states of life in general; heat and light, love and wisdom; morning, the first and highest degree of love; noon, wisdom in its light; evening, wisdom in its shade; daybreak, the obscurity which precedes the morning; and night, the deprivation of love and wisdom.

"The states of the various things without the angels, and which appear before their eyes, are also changed with the states of their interiors which are of their love and wisdom; for the things which are without them, assume an appearance corresponding to those within them.

"I have been informed from heaven why such changes of state prevail there. The angels told me there were several reasons: *First*, that the delight of life and of heaven, which results from their love and wisdom derived from the Lord, would gradually lose its value if they were always in it; as is the case with those who are in the enjoyment of delights and pleasures without variety. *Another* reason is, that angels have a proprium as well as men; that this consists in loving themselves; that all in heaven are withheld from their proprium, and are in love and wisdom so far as they are withheld from it by the Lord; but so far as they are not withheld, they are in the love of self; and because every one loves his proprium, and this draws him down, therefore they have changes of state or successive alternations. A *third* reason is, that they are perfected by these changes; for they are thus habitually held in love to the Lord, and withheld from the love of self. Their perception and sense of good is also rendered more exquisite by the alternations of delight and undelight. The angels further said, that the Lord does not produce their changes of state,— because the Lord, as a sun, is always flowing in with heat and light, that is, with love and wisdom; but that the cause is in themselves, because they love their proprium, which continually draws them away from the Lord. This they illustrated by a comparison with the sun of the world; for the changes of the state of heat and cold, of light and shade, every year and every day, do not originate in the sun, because it stands still; but they are occasioned by the motion of the earth."— Ibid. 154-158.

TIME AND SPACE IN HEAVEN.

How often is the mind so thoroughly absorbed in a subject, or so agreeably entertained by genial company, that we take no note of time. Hours pass, when to us they seem but minutes. Again, in moments of distressing anxiety, when your house is on fire, or your child has fallen into the water, seconds *seem* to you as minutes and minutes as hours. Again, do we not sometimes in our dreams have the experience of days crowded into a few moments of natural time? Do we not, in a few minutes, make journeys and accomplish deeds that would require days, weeks or months? All of which goes to prove, that, in the spiritual realm there exists not what we call time, but state instead. And now for Swedenborg's testimony on the subject. He says:

"Although all things in heaven have succession and progression as in the world, still the angels have no notion or idea of time and space, insomuch that they are altogether ignorant of what time and space are.

"They do not know what time is, — although all things with them are in successive progression as in the world, and that so completely that there is no difference, — because in heaven there are not years and days, but changes of state. And where years and days are, there are times; but where changes of state are, there are states.

"There are times in the world, because the sun of the world appears to advance successively from one degree [in the heavens] to another, thus causing the times which are called the seasons of the year; and moreover, he apparently revolves around the earth, and thus causes the times which are called times of day. Both these changes occur at regular intervals. It is otherwise with the sun of heaven. That sun does not, by successive progressions and circumgyrations, cause years and days, but, to appearance, changes of state; and these not at regular intervals.

"Hence the angels do not know what those things are which are proper to time, as a year, a month, a week, a day, an hour, to-day, to-morrow, yesterday. When they hear them named by man, they have, instead of them, a perception of states, and of such things as relate to state; thus the natural idea of man is turned into a spiritual idea with the angels. Hence it is that times in the Word signify states; and that the things which are proper to time, as those above-mentioned, signify spiritual things corresponding to them.

"The case is the same in regard to all things which exist from time, such as the four seasons of the year called spring, summer, autumn and winter; the four times of the day, called morning, noon, evening and night; the four ages of man, called infancy, youth, manhood and old age; and all other things which exist from time, or succeed according to time. In thinking of them, man thinks from time, but an angel from state. Therefore what is derived from time in the thought of man, is turned into the idea of state with an angel. Spring and morning are turned into the idea of a state of love and wisdom such as they are with the angels in their first state; summer and noon, into an idea of love and wisdom such as they are in their second state; autumn and evening, such as they are in their third state; and night and winter, into the idea of such a state as exists in hell. Hence it is that similar things are signified in the Word by those times."

Nor does our kind of space exist in the spiritual world any more than our time. Yet things appear to be in space there, precisely as in this world; and people appear to go from place to place by the exercise of their powers of locomotion, the same as on earth; but this appearance is the result of a change of state. When Paul was *caught up*, as he tells us, to the third heaven, his body underwent no change of *place*, though there was doubtless the appearance to the apostle himself of being lifted above the earth through space. In reality, he simply underwent a change of state — the interiors of his mind being opened to the third degree. And when the Lord invites us to *come unto* Him, He is to be understood spiritually, as inviting us to come into sympathy with Him — to become like Him in the spirit and temper of our minds — to pass from one *state of mind*, and not from one *place*, to another. Change of state, therefore, is spiritually denoted by change of place; and in the spiritual world the latter is the representative appearance and result of the former. Accordingly Swedenborg says:

"All progressions in the spiritual world are made by changes of the state of the interiors, so that they are nothing but changes of state. By such changes have I also been conducted by the Lord into the heavens, and likewise to the earths in the universe. I was carried there as to the spirit only, my body meanwhile remaining in the same place. Thus do all the angels journey. Hence they have no distances; and since they have no distances, they have no spaces, but instead of spaces they have states and their changes.

"Change of place being only change of state, it is evident that approximations are similitudes as to the state of the interiors, and that removals are dissimilitudes. Hence it is that those are near together who are in a similar state, and those distant who are in a dissimilar state; and that spaces in heaven are merely external states corresponding to internal. From this cause alone the heavens are distinct from each other, also the societies of each heaven, and every individual in a society. Hence, too, the hells are altogether separated from the heavens, for they are in an opposite state.

"From this cause also it is, that in the spiritual world one becomes manifestly present to another, if that other intensely desires his presence; for thus he sees him in thought, and puts himself in his state. On the other hand, one is removed from another in proportion as he holds him in aversion. All aversion is from contrariety of the affections and disagreement of the thoughts; hence it happens that many who are together in one place in the spiritual world, appear to each other so long as they agree, but disappear as soon as they disagree.

"Further: when any one goes from one place to another, whether it be in his own city, or in the courts, or in the gardens, or to others out of his own society, he arrives sooner when he desires, and later when he does not,— the distance itself being lengthened or shortened according to the desire, although it is the same. I have often observed this, and wondered at it. Hence again it is evident that distances, consequently spaces, are altogether according to the states of their interiors with the angels; and that on this account no notion or idea of space can enter their thoughts, although there are spaces with them just the same as in the world.

"Hence it is that, in the Word, by places and spaces and all things which relate to space, are signified such things as belong to state; as by distances, nearness, remoteness, ways, marches and journeyings; by miles and furlongs; by plains, fields, gardens, cities and streets; by motions; by measures of various kinds; by length, breadth, height and depth; and by innumerable other things; for most things which are in the thought of man in the world, derive something from space and time.

"From these things it may be seen, that in heaven, although there are spaces as in the world, still nothing there is estimated by spaces, but by states: consequently that spaces cannot be measured there as in the world, but only can be seen from the state and according to the state of the interiors of the angels."— Ibid. 192–198.

CORRESPONDENCE OF SPIRITUAL WITH NATURAL THINGS.

Some writer has said, "There is a language of things as well as of words." If so, things must all have a meaning, — must they not? Their visible forms must be but ultimate expressions of an invisible essence. The smile of your friend — what is it? Regarded merely as to its outward *form*, it is a peculiar disposition of the muscles of the face; but considered in reference to its *cause* or *essence*, it is a peculiar emotion of the heart. And while these two things differ widely in their *nature*, they are related, we see, like cause and effect. One produces the other; and they correspond like substance and shadow. One belongs to the mind, the other to the body. One is spiritual, the other natural. But the two things, though differing so widely in their nature, are indissolubly united, and make one by correspondence.

And according to Swedenborg, this law of correspondence is a law of creation, and of divine revelation also. The same law, therefore, is at once the key to the spiritual meaning of the Word, and determines the whole aspect of the phenomenal world in the Hereafter. He says:

"All things which exist in nature, from the least to the greatest, are correspondences. They are correspondences, because the natural world and all that belongs to it, exists and subsists from the spiritual world, and both from the Divine.

"Everything in nature which exists and subsists from divine order, is a correspondent. The divine good which proceeds from the Lord makes divine order. It commences from Him, proceeds from Him through the heavens successively into the world, and there terminates in ultimates. All things in the world which are according to order, are correspondences. Hence it is that all things in the whole world, and partaking of the nature of the world, which are in divine order, have relation to good and truth.

"That all things in the world exist from the Divine, and are appropriately clothed in nature, so as to exist there, to perform use, and thus to correspond, is manifest from everything seen both in the animal and in the vegetable kingdom. In both these kingdoms there are such things as every one, who thinks interiorly, may see to be from heaven.

"But no one at this day can know the spiritual things in heaven to which the natural things in the world correspond, except by revelation from heaven, because the knowledge of correspondences is now lost. I will therefore illustrate by some examples, the nature of the correspondence of spiritual things with natural.

"The animals of the earth in general correspond to affections; the gentle and useful ones, to good affections, the savage and useless, to evil affections. In particular, cows and oxen correspond to the affections of the natural mind; sheep and lambs, to the affections of the spiritual mind; but winged creatures, according to their species, correspond to the intellectual things of both minds. Hence it is that various animals, as cows, oxen, rams, sheep, she-goats, he-goats, he-lambs, she-lambs, and also pigeons and turtle-doves, were devoted to a sacred use in the Israelitish church,—which was a representative church,—and sacrifices and burnt-offerings were made of them; for in that use they corresponded to things spiritual, which were understood in heaven according to correspondences. Animals, also, according to their genera and species, are affections, because they live; for everything has life from no other source than from affection and according to it. Hence every animal has innate knowledge according to the affection of its life. Man, too, is similar to animals as to his natural man, and therefore is compared to them in common discourse. If he be of a gentle disposition, he is called a sheep or a lamb; if of a savage temper, he is called a bear or a wolf; if cunning, he is called a fox or a serpent; and so on.

"There is a like correspondence with the things in the vegetable kingdom. A garden in general corresponds to heaven as to intelligence and wisdom; on which account heaven is called in the Word the garden of God, and paradise, and also by man the heavenly paradise. Trees, according to their species, correspond to the perceptions and knowledges of good and truth, from which come intelligence and wisdom. Therefore the ancients, who were skilled in the knowledge of correspondences, held their sacred worship in groves; and hence it is that in the Word trees are so often mentioned, and that heaven, the church, and man, are compared to them, as to the vine, the olive, the cedar, and others; and the good works which they do, to fruits. The food also which they produce, especially that from grain, corresponds to the affections of good and truth, because these nourish the spiritual life, as terrestrial food does the natural. Hence bread in general corresponds to the affection of all good, because it supports life better than other aliments, and because bread means all kinds of food. On account of this correspondence, also, the Lord calls Himself the bread of life. And for the same reason, too, bread was applied to a sacred use in the Israelitish church; for it was set upon the table in the tabernacle, and called the bread of faces [or show-bread]; likewise all the divine worship, which was performed by sacrifices and burnt-offerings, was called bread. On account of this correspondence, also, the most holy solemnity of worship in the Christian church is the Holy Supper, in which are distributed bread and wine [bread corresponding to the good of love, and wine to the truth of wisdom]. From these few examples the nature of correspondence may be clearly seen.

"In what manner the conjunction of heaven with the world is effected by correspondences, shall also be briefly explained.

"The kingdom of the Lord is a kingdom of ends, which are uses; or,— what is the same,— it is a kingdom of uses, which are ends. Therefore the universe was so created and formed by the Divine, that uses might everywhere be clothed with coverings, whereby they are embodied in act or in effect, first in heaven and afterwards in the world; thus by degrees and successively even to the ultimates of nature. Hence it is evident that the correspondence of natural with spiritual things, or of the world with heaven, is effected by uses, and that uses conjoin them; and that the forms with which uses are clothed, are correspondences and mediums of conjunction in proportion as they are forms of use. In the natural world and its three kingdoms, all things which exist according to order are forms of use, or effects formed from use for the sake of use; therefore these things are correspondences. The actions of man likewise are uses in form, and are correspondences, whereby he is conjoined to heaven so far as he lives according to divine order, or so far as he is in love to the Lord and in charity toward his neighbor. To love the Lord and the neighbor in general is to perform uses.

"It is to be further observed, that the natural world is conjoined with the spiritual by means of man, or, that he is the medium of their conjunction; for both worlds exist in him. So far therefore as man is spiritual, he is a medium of conjunction; but so far as he is natural and not spiritual, he is not a medium of conjunction. Still, without man as a medium, the divine influx into the world continues; and also into those things which are of the world with man, but not into his rational faculty.

"As all things which are according to divine order correspond to heaven, so all things which are contrary to divine order correspond to hell. All those which correspond to heaven, have relation to good and truth; and those which correspond to hell, have relation to the evil and the false.

"Man has communication with heaven by correspondences; for the angels of heaven do not think from natural things as man does. Therefore when man is in the knowledge of correspondences, he may be associated with the angels as to the thoughts of his mind, and thus be conjoined with them as to his spiritual or internal man.

"The Word was written by pure correspondences, in order that man might be conjoined with heaven; for even the minutest parts of the Word correspond to something spiritual. Wherefore if man were skilled in the knowledge of correspondences, he would understand its spiritual sense, and become acquainted with arcana whereof he perceives nothing in the sense of the letter. For in the Word there is both a literal and a spiritual sense. The literal sense consists of such things as are in the world, but the spiritual sense of such things as are in heaven. And since the conjunction of heaven with the world is by correspondences, therefore such a Word was given, that everything in it, even to an iota, corresponds." — *Ibid.* 106–114.

HOUSES IN HEAVEN.

"Heaven is the home of the blessed," says an excellent authority. The upright and pure-hearted, when they think of heaven, think of it as a HOME — as their eternal home. Looking forward to the day of their death, they often speak of it as a time when they hope to be taken *home*.

Among the deep and strong-yearnings of every good man's heart, none, perhaps, are deeper or stronger than his yearning for a peaceful home. It is felt as a central want of the soul; and as such, we should expect that due provision would be made for its gratification in the Hereafter. God must surely provide for the ultimate satisfaction of every want which his own boundless love has implanted. And this universal desire for a home, is rooted in the constitution of the soul itself — so deeply rooted there, too, that we may be sure it will not perish with the body. And when we consider that this desire grows deeper and stronger as one advances in the life of heaven, we cannot resist the conclusion that it must exist in heaven also, and be even stronger there than here.

The angels, then, must have *homes*. But the moment we think of them as having homes, we think of them as dwelling in *houses* — so closely is the idea of home associated in our minds with some kind of habitation. The highest use of a house on earth is social or spiritual. It stands as the representative image of *home*. It is the symbol of those home-born and home-felt joys which constitute "that best portion of a good man's life."

Hear, now, what Swedenborg says on this subject:

"Since there are societies in heaven, and the angels live as men, therefore also they have habitations, and these likewise various according to every one's state of life; magnificent for those in a state of superior dignity, and less magnificent for those in an inferior condition. I have occasionally conversed with the angels concerning the habitations in heaven, and I told them that scarcely any one at this day will believe that angels have habitations and mansions; some, because they do not see them; others, because they do not know that angels are men; and others, because they believe that the angelic heaven is the heaven which they see around them; and because this appears empty, and they suppose the angels to be ethereal forms, they conclude that they live in the ether. Besides, they do not comprehend how there can be such things in the spiritual world as exist in the natural world, because they know nothing concerning what is spiritual. The angels replied, that they know such ignorance prevails in the world at this day; and to their surprise, chiefly within the church, and more among the intelligent there, than among those whom they call the simple.

"Whenever I have conversed with the angels mouth to mouth, I have been present with them in their habitations, which are exactly like the habitations on earth called houses, but more beautiful. They contain halls, parlors, and bed-chambers, in great numbers; courts also, and round about them, gardens, shrubberies and fields. Where the angels live in societies, their habitations are contiguous, close to each other, and arranged in the form of a city, with streets, courts, and public squares, exactly like the cities on our earth. I have also been permitted to walk through them, and to look around on every side, and occasionally to enter the houses. This occurred in a

8*

state of full wakefulness, when my interior sight was opened.

"I have seen the palaces of heaven, which were magnificent beyond description. Their upper parts shone refulgent as if of pure gold, and their lower parts as if of precious stones. Some were more splendid than others; and the splendor without was equalled by the magnificence within. The apartments were ornamented with decorations, which neither language nor science can adequately describe. On the side that looked to the south were paradises, where all things were equally resplendent. In some places the leaves of the trees were like silver, and the fruits like gold; and the flowers arranged in their beds presented, by their colors, the appearance of rainbows. Near the boundaries, again, appeared other palaces, which terminated the view. Such is the architecture of heaven, that one might say it is the very art itself; and no wonder, for that art itself is from heaven. The angels said that such things, and innumerable others still more perfect, are presented before their eyes by the Lord; but that, nevertheless, they delight their minds more than their eyes, because in everything they see correspondences, and by means of correspondences, things divine.

"The houses in which the angels dwell are not built like houses in the world, but are given to them gratis by the Lord,—to each one according to his reception of good and truth. They also vary a little according to the changes of the state of their interiors. All things whatsoever which the angels possess, they hold as gifts from the Lord, and they are supplied with everything they need." Ibid. 183-190.

GOVERNMENTS IN HEAVEN.

"Since heaven is distinguished into societies, and the larger societies consist of some hundreds of thousands of angels, and since all the members of one society are, indeed, in similar good, but not in similar wisdom, it necessarily follows that there are governments in heaven. For order must be observed, and all things of order are to be kept inviolable. But the governments in the heavens are various; of one sort in the societies which constitute the Lord's celestial kingdom, and of another in the societies which constitute his spiritual kingdom. They differ also according to the ministries performed by each society.

"But all the forms of government agree in this, that they regard the general good as their end, and in that, the good of every individual. This results from the fact, that all in the universal heaven are under the auspices of the Lord, who loves all, and from divine love ordains that the common good shall be the source of good to every individual; and that every individual shall receive good in proportion as he loves the common good. For so far as any one loves the community, he loves all the individuals who compose it; and since that love is the love of the Lord, therefore he is so far loved by the Lord, and good results to him.

"From these observations it may appear what is the character of the governors, namely, that they are in love and wisdom more than others; and that they will well to all from love, and from wisdom know how to provide that the good they desire may be realized. They who are of this character, do not domineer and command imperiously, but minister and serve; for to do good to others from the love of good, is to serve; and to provide that the intended good be realized, is to minister. Nor do they account themselves greater than others, but less; for they esteem the good of society and of their neighbor in the first place, but their own in the last; and what is in the first place is the greater, and what is in the last, the less.

"There are also governments in the hells; for unless there were, the infernals could not be kept under any restraint. But the governments there are the opposite of those in heaven. They are all founded in self-love; for every one there desires to rule over others and to be the greatest. They hate those who do not favor them, and pursue them with vindictiveness and cruelty, — for such is the very nature of self-love. Wherefore the most malignant are set over them as governors, whom they obey from fear." — Ibid. 213-215.

If there be houses in heaven, we should expect there would also be temples for worship. But what is the object of public or temple worship here on earth? Rightly viewed, it is to enlighten the understanding in spiritual things; to exalt the aims and purify the motives; to improve and ennoble the character; in a word, to fit us for that higher and nobler kind of worship, which consists in a religious obedience to all the known laws of the Lord and the faithful performance of every known duty. Can there be any doubt that this is the highest kind of worship, and the end aimed at in all external and formal worship? And when the worshipper has attained this end, does he not worship everywhere and at all times? — "in spirit and in truth?" Hear, now, what Swedenborg says of divine worship in heaven:

"Divine worship in heaven is not unlike that on earth as to externals, but it differs as to internals. In heaven as on earth, there are doctrines, preachings and temples. The *doctrines* agree as to essentials, but are of more interior wisdom in the superior than in the inferior heavens. The *preaching* is according to the doctrines; and as they have houses and palaces so also they have *temples* in which there is preaching. Such things exist in heaven, because the angels are continually being perfected in wisdom and love; for they have understanding and will like men, and are capable of advancing forever toward perfection. The understanding is perfected by the truths which are of intelligence, and the will by the goods which are of love.

"But real divine worship in heaven does not consist in frequenting temples and listening to sermons, but in a life of love, charity and faith according to doctrine. Sermons in the temples serve only as means of instruction in the conduct of life. I have conversed with angels on this subject, and have told them that it is believed in the world that divine worship consists merely in going to church, hearing sermons, attending the sacrament of the holy supper three or four times a year, and in other forms of worship prescribed by the church; to which may be added, the setting apart of particular times for prayer, and a devout manner while engaged in it. The angels replied, that these are externals which ought to be observed, but that they are of no avail unless there be an internal from which they proceed; and that this internal is a life according to the precepts which doctrine teaches.

"In order that I might become acquainted with their meetings in the temples, I have several times been permitted to go in and listen to the discourses. The sermons are fraught with such wisdom, that none in the world can be compared with them; for the preachers in heaven are in interior light.

"I have also conversed with one of the preachers concerning the holy state in which they are who hear the sermons in the temples; and he said that every one is in a pious, devout and holy state according to his interiors which are of love and faith, because in these is holiness itself from the Divine of the Lord; and that he had no conception of external holiness separate from love and faith. When he thought of external holiness separate from these, he said that possibly it might be something artificial or hypocritical, which simulates the outward appearance of holiness; and that some spurious fire kindled by the love of self and the world, might awaken such holiness and give it form.

"As soon as the angels hear truths, they acknowledge them, and thus perceive. The truths which they perceive, they also love; and by living according to them, they incorporate them into their lives. To live according to truths, they say, is to love the Lord.

"The doctrines preached in the temples of heaven all regard life as their end, and none of them faith without life. The doctrine of the inmost heaven is fuller of wisdom than that of the middle heaven; and the doctrine of the middle heaven is fuller of intelligence than that of the ultimate heaven; for the doctrines are adapted to the perception of the angels in each heaven. The essential of all the doctrines is, to acknowledge the Divine Human of the Lord."— Ibid. 221–227.

SPEECH OF THE ANGELS.

Do angels have a language? And do they converse together like men? Why not?— if they have mouths, tongues, ears, etc., and are perfectly human in form and feeling. The Bible, too, often speaks of them as talking and singing; and the verdict of reason accords with the teaching of revelation; and the experience of Swedenborg confirms the testimony of both. He says:

"'The angels converse together just as men do in the world, and talk, like them, on various subjects, such as domestic affairs, social affairs, and matters pertaining to moral and spiritual life. Nor is there any difference, except that they converse more intelligently than men, because from more interior thought. I have often been permitted to associate with them, and to converse with them as friend with friend, and sometimes as stranger with stranger; and because I was then in a state similar to theirs, I knew not but that I was conversing with men on earth.

"Angelic speech consists of distinct words like human speech, and is equally sonorous; for angels have a mouth, a tongue, and ears; also an atmosphere in which the sound of their speech is articulated; but it is a spiritual atmosphere accommodated to the angels, who are spiritual beings. The angels also breathe in their atmosphere, and pronounce their words by means of their breath, as men do in theirs.

"All in the whole heaven have one language, and all understand each other, whatever society they belong to, whether neighboring or remote. The language is not learned there, but is implanted in every one; for it flows from his very affection and thought. The sound of their speech corresponds to their affection, and the articulations of sound, which are words, correspond to the ideas of thought derived from affection; and because their language corresponds to these, that also is spiritual, for it is affection sounding and thought speaking.

"The wiser angels know from a single series of words what the ruling affection is; for they attend chiefly to that. Therefore they discover from his speech the whole character of the speaker. This has been proved to me by much experience. I have heard angels revealing the life of another merely from hearing him speak. They have also told me that they know the whole of another's life from a few ideas of his thought, because they learn from them his ruling love, wherein are inscribed all the particulars of his life in their order; and that man's book of life is nothing else.

"That angelic language has nothing in common with human languages, is evident from this, that it is impossible for angels to utter a single word of human language. They have tried, but were unable; for they cannot utter anything but what is in perfect agreement with their affection. Whatever is not in agreement with their affection, is repugnant to their very life; for their life is that of affection, and from this comes their speech.

"Because the speech of angels corresponds to their affection which is of love, and the love of heaven is love to the Lord and love toward the neighbor, it is obvious how elegant and delightful must be their discourse. It affects not only the ears of the listeners, but even the interiors of their minds. An angel once conversed with a certain hard-hearted spirit, who was at length so affected by his discourse that he burst into tears, saying that he could not help it, for it was love speaking; and that he had never wept before.

. "The speech of angels is also full of wisdom, because it proceeds from their interior thought; and their interior thought is wisdom, as their interior affection is love. Love and wisdom are united in their discourse; hence it is so full of wisdom, that they can express by one word what man cannot express by a thousand. The ideas of their thought also comprehend things which man cannot conceive, much less utter. Hence it is that the things which have been heard and seen in heaven are said to be ineffable, and such as ear hath not heard nor eye seen. It has also been my privilege to know from experience that this is so. I have sometimes been let into the state in which the angels are, and have conversed with them; and in that state I understood everything they said; but when I was brought back into my former state, and thus into the natural thought proper to man, and wished to recall what I had heard, I was unable; for there were a thousand things which could not be brought down to the ideas of natural thought, and therefore could not be at all expressed in human language.

"Speech similar to that in the spiritual world is inherent in every man, but in his interior intellectual part. But man does not know this, because it does not fall into words analogous to his affection, as it does with the angels. Yet it is from this cause that man, when he comes into the other life, speaks the language of spirits and angels without effort or instruction.

"All in heaven speak the same language, as was said above; but it varies in this respect, that the speech of the wise is more interior, and fuller of the variations of affection and of the ideas of thoughts."— *Ibid.* 234–244.

DANGER IN SPEAKING WITH SPIRITS.

At this day, when so many are *prying into* the spiritual world through modern "mediums," so called, instead of heeding the revelation that God has been pleased to make, the following remarks by Swedenborg upon the danger of this practice, ought not to be passed over:

"To speak with spirits at this day is rarely permitted, because it is dangerous; for the spirits then know that they are present with man, which they otherwise do not. And evil spirits are of such a nature that they regard man with deadly hatred, and desire nothing more than to destroy him, both soul and body. This also they accomplish with those who have indulged much in fantasies, so as to remove from themselves the delights suitable to the natural man. Yet some who lead a solitary life occasionally hear spirits speaking with them, and without danger.

"Persons who think much upon religious subjects, and are so intent upon them as to see them as it were inwardly in themselves, also begin to hear spirits speaking with them; for religious subjects of whatever kind — when a man of his own accord dwells upon them, and does not interrupt the current of his thoughts by various uses in the world — penetrate interiorly, become fixed there, occupy the whole spirit of the man, and in fact enter into the spiritual world and act upon the spirits who dwell there. But such persons are visionaries and enthusiasts, and believe whatever spirit they hear to be the Holy Spirit, when yet they are enthusiastic spirits. Such spirits see falsities as truths, and because they see them, they persuade themselves that they are truths, and infuse the same persuasion into those who are receptive of their influx.

"Enthusiastic spirits are distinguished from other spirits by this peculiarity, that they believe themselves to be the Holy Spirit, and their sayings divine. They do not hurt the man with whom they communicate, because he honors them with divine worship. I have also several times conversed with these spirits; and on such occasions the wicked principles and motives which they infused into their worshipers were discovered.

"But to speak with the angels of heaven is granted only to those who are in truth derived from good, and especially to those who are in the acknowledgment of the Lord, and of the Divine in his Human, because this is the truth wherein the heavens are established."— Ibid. 249, 250.

THE WISDOM OF THE ANGELS.

"What the wisdom of the angels is may be concluded from the fact that they dwell in the light of heaven; and the light of heaven in its essence is divine truth, or divine wisdom; and this light enlightens at the same time their internal sight, which is that of the mind, and their external sight which is that of the eyes. All things which they see with their eyes and perceive by their senses, are in agreement with their wisdom, because they are correspondences, and thence forms representative of such things as belong to wisdom.

"How great the wisdom of the angels is, may be further evident from the fact, that in heaven there is a communication of all things,— the intelligence and wisdom of one being communicated to another. Heaven is a communion of all good things, because heavenly love wills that what is its own should be another's; consequently no one in heaven perceives his own good in himself as good, unless it be also in another. Thence also is the happiness of heaven. The angels derive from the Lord this disposition to communicate, for such is the nature of the Divine Love. That there is such communication in the heavens, has also been given me to know by experience. Certain simple spirits were once taken up into heaven; and when there, they came also into angelic wisdom, and then understood things which they could not comprehend before, and spoke such things as they were unable to utter in their former state.

"The wisdom of the angels in comparison with human wisdom, is as a myriad to one, — comparatively as the moving forces of the whole body, which are innumerable, are to the action resulting from them, wherein to human sense they appear as one ; or as the thousand things pertaining to an object as seen through a perfect microscope, to the one obscure thing which it appears to the naked eye. To illustrate the subject by an example :

"An angel from his wisdom explained regeneration, and made known arcana concerning it in their order even to some hundreds, filling each one with ideas which contained arcana still more interior, — and this from beginning to end ; for he explained how the spiritual man is conceived anew, is carried as it were in the womb, is born, grows up, and is successively perfected. He said that he could increase the number of arcana even to some thousands ; and that he had only mentioned those concerning the regeneration of the external man, and that there were innumerably more concerning the regeneration of the internal. From this and other similar examples which I have heard from the angels, it was made manifest to me how great is their wisdom, and how great, respectively, the ignorance of man.

"The angels of the inmost heaven never reason about divine truths, still less do they dispute about any truth, whether it be so or not so ; nor do they know what it is to believe or have faith. They say, What is faith? for I perceive and see that it is so. This they illustrate by comparisons, saying, that, to urge a man to have faith, who sees the truth in himself, is like saying to one who sees a house and the various things in and around it, that he ought to have faith in them, and believe that they are just as he sees; or it is like telling a man who sees a garden with its trees and fruits, that he ought to have faith that it is a garden, and that the trees and fruits are trees and fruits, when yet he sees them plainly with his own eyes.

"The angels of the inmost heaven do not store up divine truths in the memory; thus they do not make anything like a science of them; but as soon as they hear them they perceive them to be truths, and commit them to life. Divine truths therefore remain with them as if inscribed on their interiors; for what is committed to the life thus abides internally. But it is otherwise with the angels of the lowest heaven.

"An additional reason — which also is the primary one in heaven — why the angels are capable of receiving such exalted wisdom, is, because they are free from self-love; for in proportion as any one is free from that love, he is capable of becoming wise in things divine. It is that love which closes the interiors against the Lord and heaven, and opens the exteriors and turns them toward self. Wherefore all those with whom that love predominates are in thick darkness as to the things of heaven, however enlightened they may be as to those of the world. But angels on the other hand, because they are free from self-love, are in the light of wisdom; for the heavenly loves in which they are, which are love to the Lord and love toward the neighbor, open the interiors; because those loves are from the Lord, and the Lord Himself is in them.

"The angels are continually perfecting in wisdom; but yet they cannot to eternity be so far perfected, that there can be any ratio between their wisdom and the divine wisdom of the Lord; for the divine wisdom of the Lord is infinite, and between the infinite and the finite there is no ratio." — Ibid. 266–273.

ANGELIC INNOCENCE.

"The innocence of infancy, or of little children, is not genuine innocence, for it exists only in the external form, and not in the internal. Nevertheless we may learn from that what innocence is, for it shines forth from their faces, from some of their gestures, and from their earliest speech, and affects those around them. The reason is that they have no internal thought; for they do not yet know what is good or evil, nor what is true or false; and from these, thought is derived.

"'The innocence of wisdom is genuine innocence, because it is internal; for it belongs to the mind itself, thus to the will itself, and thence to the understanding;

and when innocence is in these, there is also wisdom, for wisdom pertains to the will and understanding. Hence it is said in heaven that innocence dwells in wisdom, and that an angel has as much of wisdom as he has of innocence. That such is the case, they confirm by this: that those who are in a state of innocence attribute nothing of good to themselves, but regard all their goods as gifts received, and ascribe them to the Lord; that they wish to be led by Him, and not by themselves; that they love everything which is good, and are delighted with everything which is true; because they know and perceive that to love what is good, thus to will and to do it, is to love the Lord; and to love what is true, is to love their neighbor; that they live contented with their own, whether it be little or much, because they know that they receive as much as is profitable for them; little, if little be profitable, and much, if much be profitable; and that they do not themselves know what is best for them, this being known only to the Lord, whose providence in all things contemplates eternal ends. Hence they are not anxious about the future. They call solicitude about the future, care for the morrow, which they say is grief for the loss or non-reception of things which are not necessary for the uses of life. In their intercourse with others they never act from an evil end, but from what is good, just and sincere. To act from an evil end they call cunning, which they shun as the poison of a serpent, since it is altogether contrary to innocence. Because they love nothing more than to be led of the Lord, and acknowledge their indebtedness to Him for everything they receive, therefore they are removed from their proprium; and in the degree that they are removed from their proprium, in the same degree the Lord flows-in. Hence it is, that whatever they hear from Him, whether through the medium of the Word or of preaching, they do not store up in the memory, but immediately obey; that is, they will and do it, — the will itself being their memory.

"Because innocence consists in being led by the Lord and not by self, therefore all who are in heaven are in innocence; for all who are there love to be led by the Lord. They know, indeed, that to lead themselves, is to be led by the proprium, and the proprium consists in loving one's self; and he who loves himself, does not permit another to lead him. Hence it is, that as far as an angel is in innocence he is in heaven, that is, in divine good and divine truth; for to be in these is to be in heaven. The heavens, therefore, are distinguished according to innocence."—Ibid. 277-280.

HEAVENLY PEACE.

"He who has not experienced the peace of heaven, can have no conception of that which the angels enjoy in heaven. Peace is the Divine inmostly affecting with blessedness every good there; yea, it is the source of all the joy of heaven; and in its essence it is the divine joy of the Lord's divine love, resulting from the conjunction of Himself with heaven and with every one there. This joy — perceived by the Lord in angels, and by angels from the Lord — is peace. Hence by derivation the angels have all that is blessed, delightful and happy, or that which is called heavenly joy.

"Innocence and peace dwell together like good and its delight, as may be seen in the case of little children, who, because they are in innocence, are also in peace; and because they are in peace, therefore they are full of playfulness; but their peace is external; for internal peace, like internal innocence, is not given except in wisdom, and therefore in the conjunction of good and truth, — for this is the origin of wisdom. Heavenly or angelic peace exists also with men who are in wisdom from the conjunction of good and truth, and are thence conscious of content in God; yet while they live in the world, that peace lies stored up in their interiors, but is revealed when they leave the body and enter heaven; for then the interiors are opened.

"I have conversed with the angels about peace; and I remarked that it is called peace in the world, when wars and hostilities cease between kingdoms, and when enmity and discord cease among men; and that internal peace is believed to consist in a repose of mind arising from the removal of cares, and especially in tranquillity and delight from success in business. But the angels said, that repose of mind, and tranquillity and delight arising from the removal of cares and from success in business, appear to be the constituents of peace, but are not so, except with those who are in heavenly good, since there is no peace except in that good; for peace flows-in from the Lord into the inmost degree of their minds, and from their inmost it descends and flows down into the lower degrees, and produces repose of the rational mind [*mens*], tranquillity of the natural mind [*animus*] and joy thence.

"But they who are in evil have no peace. There appears, indeed, something like rest, tranquillity, and delight, when things succeed according to their wishes, but it is external and not internal; for internally they burn with enmity, hatred, revenge, cruelty, and many other evil lusts, into which their external mind also rushes — bursting forth into violence if unrestrained by fear — the moment they see any one who is not favorable to them." — Ibid. 284-290.

ANGELS AND DEVILS FROM THE HUMAN RACE.

Creation commences on the lowest plane, and advances steadily upward. That which is first in the order of importance, is always last in the order of time. The stem and leaves come before the fruit. The child precedes the man; and the lowest and sensuous part of our nature unfolds before the rational and spiritual. And, by parity of reasoning, we may conclude that heaven is but the full unfolding of earth, and angels but perfected men. Therefore all in the spiritual world should have commenced their existence on earth. Reason and analogy force upon us this conclusion. And with this conclusion accords the testimony of Swedenborg. He says:

"It is altogether unknown in the Christian world that heaven and hell are from the human race; for it is believed that angels were created from the beginning, and that this was the origin of heaven; and that the devil or satan was an angel of light, but because he became rebellious, he was cast down with his crew; and that this was the origin of hell. The angels wonder very much that such a belief should prevail in the Christian world, and still more that nothing whatever is known about heaven, when yet it is a primary point of doctrine in the church. Therefore they desire me to declare positively from their mouths, that there is not a single angel in the universal heaven who was originally created such, nor any devil in hell who was created an angel of light and cast down; but that all, both in heaven and in hell, are from the human race; in heaven, those who lived in the world in heavenly love and faith; in hell, those who lived in infernal love and faith; and that hell in the whole complex is what is called the devil and satan.

"That heaven is from the human race may be further evident from this, that angelic minds and human minds are similar. Both enjoy the faculty of understanding, perceiving and willing. Both are formed to receive heaven; for the human mind is capable of wisdom as well as the angelic mind; but it does not become so wise in the world, because it is in an earthly body, and in that the spiritual mind thinks naturally. But it is otherwise when released from its connection with that body. Then it no longer thinks naturally, but spiritually; and when it thinks spiritually, then it thinks things incomprehensible and ineffable to the natural man; thus it becomes wise as an angel."—Ibid. 311, 314.

But this, as you well know, is very different from the doctrine on this subject generally accepted a hundred years ago.

A HEAVEN FOR GENTILES.

The theologians of Swedenborg's day were quite unanimous in the opinion that, without a knowledge and belief of the Christian Scriptures, salvation is not possible. But not many intelligent Christians, nowadays, really believe that the millions who are born and die in heathen lands, are to "perish everlastingly." Such an idea is shocking. And what a monster of cruelty would it show the Creator of these millions to be! How much more agreeable to both the dictates of enlightened reason and the teachings of Holy Scripture, is the following explicit testimony of Swedenborg:

"It is a common opinion that those who are born out

of the church, who are called Heathen or Gentiles, cannot be saved; because they have not the Word, and thus are ignorant of the Lord, without whom there can be no salvation. Nevertheless it may be known that they also are saved, from these considerations alone: That the mercy of the Lord is universal, that is, extended toward every individual; that they are born men as well as those within the church, who are respectively few; and that it is no fault of theirs that they are ignorant of the Lord. Every person who thinks from any enlightened reason, may see that no man is born for hell; for the Lord is love itself, and it is agreeable to his love that all be saved. Wherefore also He has provided that all shall have some kind of religion, and thereby be in the acknowledgment of a Divine, and in the enjoyment of interior life: for to live according to religion is to live interiorly; for then man looks up to a Divine.

"That Gentiles are saved as well as Christians, may be known to those who understand what it is that makes heaven in man. For heaven is in man, and those who have heaven in themselves enter heaven after death. It is heaven in man to acknowledge a Divine, and to be led by Him. The first and primary thing of every religion is, to acknowledge a Divine. A religion which does not include this acknowledgment, is no religion at all. And the precepts of every religion have respect to worship; thus they teach how the Divine is to be worshiped in a manner acceptable to Him; and when this is settled in one's mind, yea, in the degree that he wills or loves it, in that degree he is led by the Lord. It is known that Gentiles live a moral life as well as Christians; and that many of them live better than Christians. Men live a moral life either for the sake of the Divine, or from a regard to the opinion of the world. The moral life which is lived for the sake of the Divine is spiritual life.

"I have often been instructed that Gentiles who have led a moral life, have lived in obedience and subordination, and in mutual charity according to their religion, and have therefore received something of conscience, are accepted in the other life, and are there instructed with anxious care by angels in the goods and truths of faith; and that, while under instruction, they behave themselves modestly, intelligently and wisely, and willingly receive truths, and are imbued with them; besides, they have formed to themselves no principles of the false contrary to the truths of faith, which are to be shaken off, much less scandals against the Lord, — like many Christians who cherish no other idea of Him than that of a common man. It is a divine truth, that without the Lord there is no salvation; but this is to be understood to mean that there is no salvation but from the Lord. There are many earths in the universe, and all of them full of inhabitants. Scarcely any there know that the Lord assumed the Human on our earth. Nevertheless, because they adore the Divine under a human form, they are accepted and led of the Lord.

"The church of the Lord is spread over the whole terrestrial globe, and is thus universal. It embraces all who have lived in the good of charity according to their religious belief. And the church where the Word is, and where by means of it the Lord is known, is, to those who are out of the church, as the heart and lungs in man, from which all the viscera and members of the body live variously according to their forms, situations and connections."—Ibid. 318-328.

CHILDREN IN HEAVEN.

Not only did Christians, a hundred years ago, generally believe and teach that the millions who die in Heathen lands unconverted to Christianity, are doomed to a state of everlasting torment, but the equally unreasonable and monstrous doctrine of the eternal damnation of multitudes dying in infancy and childhood, was as generally taught and accepted for the truth. You, doubtless, are sufficiently familiar with the religious beliefs of that period, to know that this dogma was then held by every branch of the Christian church, both Protestant and Catholic. If you are not, I refer you to Part I. of my little work entitled "Beauty for Ashes," wherein you will find abundant authorities cited or referred to in justification of this statement.

But no Christian minister ever thinks of preaching this doctrine nowadays, however fairly it may be deduced from some other portions of his creed; or, if he should, he would, I doubt not, soon be compelled to preach it to vacant pews. No enlightened congregation would listen to it. It is the universal belief of the churches now, that all who die in infancy and childhood, go among the blest and are eternally happy. And you and I and all others rejoice at this. We hail it as one of the signs of religious progress. But what has wrought this universal change of sentiment? Who first advanced the idea that all who die in infancy and childhood, go to heaven? Emanuel Swedenborg — the man whose heavenly mission is as generally discredited by the Christian teachers of our day, as was the mission of Christ by the Jewish teachers eighteen centuries ago. In his chapter on "Infants in Heaven," written one hundred and fourteen years ago, he says:

"Some believe that only the infants who are born within the church go to heaven, but not those born out of the church; and the reason they assign is, that infants within the church are baptized, and are thus initiated into the faith of the church. But they are not aware that no one receives heaven or faith by baptism, for baptism is only for a sign and memorial that man is to be regenerated; and that he can be regenerated who is born within the church, since there is the Word which contains the divine truths by means of which regeneration is effected; there also the Lord is known, by whom it is accomplished. Be it known, therefore, that every infant, wheresoever born, — whether within the church or out of it, whether of pious or impious parents, — when he dies, is received by the Lord, and educated in heaven. He is there instructed according to divine order, and is imbued with affections of good, and by them with the knowledge of truth; and afterward, as he is perfected in intelligence and wisdom, he is introduced into heaven and becomes an angel.

"Every one after his decease, is in a similar state of life to that in which he was in the world: an infant in a state of infancy; a boy in a state of boyhood; a youth, a man, an old man, in the state of a youth, of a man, and of an old man. But the state of every one is afterwards changed. The state of infants, however, excels that of all others in this respect, that they are in innocence, and evil from actual life has not yet taken root in them. And such is the nature of innocence, that all things of heaven may be implanted in it; for it is the receptacle of the truth of faith and of the good of love.

"As soon as infants are raised from the dead, which takes place immediately after their decease, they are taken into heaven, and committed to the care of angels of the female sex, who in the life of the body loved little children tenderly, and at the same time loved God. Because these angels when in the world loved all infants from a sort of maternal tenderness, they receive them as their own; and the little ones also, from an inclination implanted in them, love them as their own mothers."

Observe, too, that the reported method of teaching little children in the other world, is the very same as that recently adopted by the best educators here on earth, and known as "the object method."

"How infants are educated in heaven shall also be briefly told. Into their affections, which all proceed from innocence, are first insinuated such things as appear before their eyes, and are delightful; and as these are from a spiritual origin, the things of heaven flow into them at the same time, by means of which their interiors are opened; and thus they become more perfect every day. They are instructed chiefly by representatives suited to their capacities, which are so beautiful, and at the same time so full of wisdom from an interior ground, as to exceed all belief.

"Many persons may imagine that infants remain such in heaven, and exist as infants among the angels. They who do not know what constitutes an angel, may have confirmed themselves in this opinion from the images sometimes seen in churches, where angels are exhibited as infants. But the case is altogether otherwise. Intelligence and wisdom constitute an angel; and so long as infants have not intelligence and wisdom, they are not angels, although they are with angels. But when they become intelligent and wise, then for the first time they become angels. Yea,—a thing that I have wondered at, — they then no longer appear as infants, but as adults; for they are then no longer of an infantile genius, but of a more mature angelic genius. Intelligence and wisdom produce this effect. As infants are perfected in intelligence and wisdom, they appear more mature, thus as youths and young men, because intelligence and wisdom are real spiritual nourishment. For this reason the things which nourish their minds nourish their bodies also,— and this from correspondence; for the form of the body is but the external form of the interiors. It is to be observed that infants in heaven do not advance in age beyond the period of early manhood; and there they stop forever [*i. e.* so far as apparent progress in *age* is concerned].

"Little children [in heaven] do not know that they were born in the world, but think that they were born in heaven. Consequently they know nothing of any birth but the spiritual birth, which is effected by the knowledge of good and truth, and by intelligence and wisdom, by virtue of which man is man; and because these are from the Lord, they believe and love to believe that they are the children of the Lord Himself.

"Nevertheless the state of men who grow up on earth, may become just as perfect as the state of those who grow up in heaven from a state of infancy, provided they remove corporeal and terrestrial loves—which are the loves of self and the world—and in their place receive spiritual loves."—Ibid. 329–345.

If we accept the teaching of Scripture according to the sense of the letter, we must believe that a rich man can never enter heaven; for we read that, "it is easier for a camel to go through the eye of a needle, than for a rich man to enter into the kingdom of God;"—which is equivalent to saying that the entrance of such a man into that kingdom, is utterly out of the question. Yet the eagerness with which even religious people strive to amass wealth, proves that there is (as well there may be) an almost universal distrust of the literal verity of this Scripture. The following is the sensible way in which Swedenborg writes on the subject:

"There are various opinions about reception into heaven. Some suppose that the poor are received and not the rich; others, that the rich and poor are received alike; and others, that the rich cannot be received unless they give up their wealth and become as the poor; and each proves his opinion from the Word.

"But they who make a distinction between the rich and poor as to their facility of admission into heaven, do not understand the Word. The Word in its bosom is spiritual, but in the letter it is natural. Therefore they who take the Word merely according to its literal and not according to its spiritual sense, err upon many points; as, in supposing that it is as difficult for the rich to enter heaven as for a camel to go through the eye of a needle; and that it is easy for the poor because they are poor, since it is said: *'Blessed are the poor, for theirs is the kingdom of heaven.'* Matt. v. 3; Luke vi. 20, 21. But they who know anything of the spiritual sense of the Word, are of a different opinion.

" From much conversation and intercourse with the angels, it has been granted me to know for a certainty that the rich enter heaven as easily as the poor; that no man is excluded on account of his great possessions, and that no one is received because he is poor. Both rich and poor are there.

" A man may acquire riches as far as opportunity is given him, provided it be not done with craft and dishonesty; he may eat and drink daintily, provided he does not make life consist in that; he may dwell magnificently according to his condition; he may converse with others as others do; he may frequent places of amusement, and talk about worldly affairs; and has no need to assume a devout aspect, to be of a sad and sorrowful countenance, and to bow down his head, but may be glad and cheerful.

"And these things will not prevent his going to heaven, provided that inwardly in himself he thinks properly about God, and acts sincerely and justly with his neighbor. For man is such as his affection and thought are, or such as his love and faith are. All his outward acts derive their life from these; for to act is to will, and to speak is to think, since every one acts from will and speaks from thought.

"Hence it may be manifest that the love of riches, and of the uses to be performed by riches, remains with every one to eternity, and that it is altogether such as was procured in the world; yet with this difference, that with those who had employed them in the promotion of good uses, riches are turned into delights according to the uses; but with those who had employed them in the promotion of evil uses, they are turned into filth. Then also the evil are delighted with such filth, in like manner as in the world they were delighted with riches for the sake of evil uses. They are then delighted with filth, because the filthy pleasures and infamies which were the uses to which they applied their riches, and also avarice, which is the love of riches without regard to use, correspond to filth. Spiritual filth is nothing else.

"The poor do not go to heaven on account of their poverty, but on account of their life. Every one's life [*i. e.* his character] follows him, whether he be rich or poor. There is no peculiar mercy for one more than for another. He who has lived well is received, and he who has lived ill is rejected.

"Besides, poverty seduces and withdraws man from heaven as much as wealth. Great numbers among the poor are not contented with their lot, but are eager after many things, and believe riches to be blessings. They are angry, therefore, when they do not receive them, and think evil concerning the Divine Providence. They also envy others the good things which they possess.

Besides, they are as ready as the wicked among the rich to defraud others, and to live in sordid pleasures when they have the opportunity. But it is otherwise with the poor who are content with their lot, who are faithful and diligent in their calling, who love labor better than idleness, who act sincerely and honestly, and live a Christian life."— Ibid. 357–364.

MARRIAGES IN HEAVEN.

The prevailing idea among Christians a hundred years ago, was, that sex cannot be predicated of the soul; and that, consequently, there are no sexes in the other world; and hence there can be no marriages there. But the unreasonableness of this is every day becoming more and more apparent to thoughtful minds. Reflecting people in all the churches are coming to see the absurdity of supposing that the death of the body will destroy the distinction of sex, or work any change in it whatever. The truth is beginning to be widely accepted, that man and woman differ not a whit less in their souls than in their bodies; that sex belongs to the former as much as to the latter; that they are the complements of each other, and necessary to each other's wholeness. If this be reasonable, then is it not equally reasonable that marriages should take place in heaven?—more blissful and perfect, too, than most of the marriages on earth, because between regenerate souls, who from their very constitution are the complements of each other, and each therefore necessary to the other's completeness.*

Hear, now, the testimony of Swedenborg, who is not giving us *his opinion*, remember, but speaks "from things heard and seen."

"Because heaven is from the human race, and the angels of heaven are therefore of both sexes; and because it was ordained from creation that the woman should be for the man and the man for the woman, and thus that each should be the other's; and because this love is innate in both; it follows that there are marriages in heaven as well as on earth. But marriages in heaven are very different from those on earth.

"Marriage in heaven is the conjoining of two into one mind. What this conjunction is shall be explained. The mind consists of two parts, one of which is called the understanding, the other the will. When these two parts act in unity, they are then called one mind. In heaven the husband acts that part which is called the understanding, and the wife that which is called the will. When this conjunction, which is of the interiors, descends into the inferiors, which are of the body, it is perceived

---

* Our Saviour's language to the Sadducees may seem in conflict with this; and in its literal sense, or as commonly understood, it unquestionably is. But those who desire to know the spiritual and true meaning of the words, "For in the resurrection they neither marry nor are given in marriage," &c., are referred to an interesting work by Dr. W. H. Holcombe, entitled "The Sexes Here and Hereafter," Chapter III. — where they will find it fully explained.

and felt as love. This love is conjugial love. Hence it is evident, that conjugial love derives its origin from the conjunction of two into one mind. This is called in heaven cohabitation; and it is said that they are not two but one. Therefore two married partners in heaven are not called two but one angel.

"That there is also such a conjunction of husband and wife in the inmosts of their minds, results from creation itself; for the man is born to be intellectual, thus to think from the understanding; but the woman is born to be voluntary, thus to think from the will.

"Every one — man as well as woman — possesses understanding and will; but still with the man the understanding predominates, and with the woman the will; and the character of a person is determined by that which predominates. But in marriages in heaven there is no predominance; for the will of the wife is also that of the husband, and the understanding of the husband is also that of the wife; since each loves to will and to think as the other, thus mutually and reciprocally. Hence their conjunction into one. From these considerations it may be manifest that the conjunction of minds, which makes marriage and produces conjugial love in heaven, consists in this: that each one wishes all he has to be the other's; and this reciprocally.

"I have been told by the angels, that as far as two married partners are in such conjunction, they are in conjugial love; and at the same time in the like degree in intelligence, wisdom and happiness, because divine good and divine truth, from which all intelligence, wisdom and happiness are derived, flow principally into conjugial love; consequently that conjugial love is the very plane of the divine influx.

"I once heard an angel describing love truly conjugial and its heavenly delights, in this manner: that it is the Divine of the Lord in heaven — which is the divine good and the divine truth — united in two beings, yet in such a manner that they are not two but as one. He said that two conjugial partners in heaven are that love — because every one is his own good and his own truth — with respect to mind as well as body; for the body is the effigy of the mind, because formed in its likeness. Hence he concluded that the Divine is effigied in two, who are in love truly conjugial. And because the Divine is effigied in them, so also is heaven,— for the universal heaven is the divine good and the divine truth proceeding from the Lord; and that hence all things of heaven are inscribed on that love, with beatitudes and delights more than can be numbered. He expressed the number by a term which involves myriads of myriads.

"They are in conjugial love who are in divine good from divine truths; and conjugial love is so far genuine as the truths which are conjoined to good are genuine. And because all good which is conjoined to truths is from the Lord, it follows that no one can be in love truly conjugial, unless he acknowledge the Lord and his Divine; for without this acknowledgment the Lord cannot flow-in, and be conjoined with the truths which are with man.

" From these remarks it is evident that they are not in conjugial love who are in falsities, and still less they who are in falsities derived from evil.

" Nor is love truly conjugial possible between one husband and more wives than one; for this destroys its spiritual origin, which is the formation of one mind out of two; consequently it destroys interior conjunction, which is that of good and truth, from which is the very essence of conjugial love. Marriage with more than one wife is like an understanding divided among more wills than one; and like a man who is attached to more churches than one, whereby his faith is so distracted that it becomes no faith. The angels say, that to have a plurality of wives is altogether contrary to divine order; and that they know this from many causes; and from this among others, that as soon as they think of marriage with more than one, they are estranged from internal blessedness and heavenly felicity.

"The love of exercising dominion one over the other, completely takes away conjugial love and its heavenly delight; for, as was said above, conjugial love and its delight consist in this, that the will of one be that of the other, and this mutually and reciprocally. The love of dominion in marriage destroys this; for he who domineers wishes that his will alone should be in the other, and none of the other's reciprocally in himself; hence there is nothing mutual, consequently no reciprocal communication of one's love and its delight with the other; yet this communication, and thence conjunction, is the interior delight itself in marriage, which is called blessedness. The love of dominion completely extinguishes this blessedness, and with it all celestial and spiritual love.

"Marriages in heaven differ from marriages on earth in this respect: that, besides other uses, marriages on earth are for the procreation of offspring, but not in heaven; there, instead of such procreation, there is the procreation of good and truth. This procreation is instead of the former, because marriage in heaven is the marriage of good and truth,—as was shown above,—and in that marriage, good and truth and their conjunction are loved above all else; these, therefore, are what are propagated from marriages in heaven. Hence it is that by nativities and generations in the Word are signified spiritual nativities and generations, which are those of good and truth.

" How marriages are contracted in heaven, I have also been allowed to see. Everywhere in heaven those who are alike are associated, and those who are unlike are dissociated. Hence every society of heaven consists of like ones. They who are alike are brought together, not of themselves but of the Lord. In like manner conjugial partners, whose minds are capable of being conjoined into one, are drawn together. Therefore at first sight they deeply love each other, and see that they are conjugial partners, and enter into marriage. Hence it is that all the marriages in heaven are of the Lord alone. They also hold a festival on the occasion, which is attended by a numerous company. The festivities differ in different societies.

"The angels regard marriages on earth as most holy, because they are the seminaries of the human race, and also of the angels of heaven, — for, as was shown above in its proper chapter, heaven is from the human race; also because they are from a spiritual origin, namely, from the marriage of good and truth; and because the Divine of the Lord flows primarily into conjugial love. And on the other hand, they regard adulteries as profane, because they are contrary to conjugial love; for as in marriages the angels behold the marriage of good and truth, which is heaven, so in adulteries they behold the marriage of the false and evil, which is hell. Therefore when they only hear adultery mentioned, they turn themselves away. This also is the reason why heaven is closed against a man when he commits adultery from delight; and when heaven is closed, he no longer acknowledges the Divine, nor anything pertaining to the faith of the church.

"That all who are in hell are in opposition to conjugial love, it has been given me to perceive from the sphere thence exhaling, which was like a perpetual endeavor to dissolve and violate marriages. From this it was evident that the ruling delight in hell is the delight of adultery; and that the delight of adultery is also the delight of destroying the conjunction of good and truth, which conjunction makes heaven. Hence it follows that the delight of adultery is an infernal delight, altogether opposed to the delight of marriage, which is a heavenly delight."

Tell me, my brother — Does this sound like the utterances of a dreamer? — or fanatic? — or one who has lost his mental balance? Can you point me to any higher wisdom touching the relation of the sexes and the nature of true marriage, than is contained in these few paragraphs? Where, in the whole range of Christian literature prior to Swedenborg's time, will you find anything to compare with this? Is it not altogether worthy of the origin claimed for it?

EMPLOYMENTS IN HEAVEN.

One hundred years ago, Christians were taught to believe that the principal occupation of the saints in heaven was, preaching or listening to sermons, singing psalms and praying. Think of spending an eternity in this manner! And then what valuable purpose could it subserve? Would it add to the greatness or glory of God? — or promote the happiness of his children in heaven or on earth? God desires our prayers and songs of praise, not for *his* glory, but for *our own* good; and they are useful as a means of bringing our souls into nearness and sympathy with Him. But let any one engage in praying and singing as a constant employment, and let him pursue it steadily for three weeks — or even one — and he will, I think, be disabused of the notion that verbal prayers and songs of praise are the chief occupation of the angels. He will learn from this brief experience the utter falsity of such an idea, — unless the laws of the soul and the conditions of happiness are to be totally different in the Hereafter from what they are here. And he will be ready, I think, to accept the following disclosures by Swedenborg on this subject, as far more reasonable, as well as more profitable to the believer — more important and healthy in their practical tendency :

"It is impossible to enumerate or describe specifically the employments of heaven, for they are innumerable and various according to the offices of the societies. Every one there performs a use; for the kingdom of the Lord is a kingdom of uses.

"There are in heaven as on earth various administrations; for there are there ecclesiastical, civil and domestic affairs. And there are many employments and administrations in every heavenly society.

"The wiser angels take charge of those things belonging to the general good or use, and the less wise, of those relating to particular goods or uses; and so on. They are subordinated, just as in divine order uses are subordinated. Hence also dignity is attached to every employment according to the dignity of the use. No angel, however, arrogates the dignity to himself, but ascribes it all to the use; and because use is the good which he does, and all good is from the Lord, therefore he ascribes it all to the Lord. Wherefore he who thinks of honor for himself and thence for use, and not for use and thence for himself, cannot perform any office in heaven; because he looks backward from the Lord, regarding himself in the first place and use in the second.

"There are societies in heaven whose employment consists in taking care of infants; others whose employment is to instruct and educate them as they grow up; others who instruct and educate boys and girls of a good disposition from education in the world; others who teach the simple good from the Christian world, and lead them in the way to heaven; others who perform the same office for the various Gentile nations; others who defend novitiate spirits — those who have recently come from the world — from infestations by evil spirits; and some also who attend upon those who are being raised from the dead. In general, angels of every society are sent to men, that they may guard them, and withdraw them from evil affections and consequent evil thoughts, and inspire them with good affections so far as they receive them freely. By means of these affections also they rule the deeds or works of men, removing from them evil intentions as far as possible. But all these employments of the angels are functions performed by the Lord through them; for the angels perform them, not from themselves, but from the Lord.

"Ecclesiastical affairs in heaven are under the charge of those who, when in the world, loved the Word, and earnestly sought for the truths which it contains, not for the sake of honor or gain, but for the sake of the use of life, both their own and others. These are in illustration and in the light of wisdom in heaven according to their love and desire of use; for they come into that light in the heavens from the Word, which is not natural there as in the world, but spiritual. These perform the office of preachers.

"Civil affairs are administered by those who, while in the world, loved their country and its general good in preference to their own; and who did what is just and right from the love of justice and rectitude. Such men possess capacity for administering offices in heaven, in proportion as their love of rectitude has prompted them to inquire into the laws of justice, and thence to become intelligent. The offices which they administer correspond exactly to the degree of their intelligence; and their intelligence is then in like degree also with their love of use for the general good.

"There are so many offices and administrations in heaven, and so many employments also, that it is impossible to enumerate them on account of their multitude. Those in the world are comparatively few. All, how many soever there be, are in the delight of their occupation, and labor from the love of use, and no one from the love of self or gain. Nor is any one influenced by the love of gain for the sake of maintenance, because all the necessaries of life are given them gratis, — their habitations, garments and food. Hence it is evident that they who have loved themselves and the world more than use, have no lot in heaven; for every one's own love or affection remains with him after his life in the world, nor is it extirpated to eternity.

"Every one in heaven is in his work according to correspondence; and the correspondence is not with the work, but with the use of every work; and there is a correspondence of all things. He who is in an employment or work in heaven corresponding to his use, is in a state of life exactly like that in which he was in the world, — for what is spiritual and what is natural act as one by correspondence — but with this difference: that he is in more interior delight, because in spiritual life which is interior life; hence he is more receptive of heavenly blessedness." — Ibid. 387–394.

THE HAPPINESS OF HEAVEN.

In his last but one chapter of the work on "Heaven and its Wonders," Swedenborg treats of "Heavenly Joy and Happiness." As if he had said, "Here I give you the final outcome or sum total of all that heavenly order and economy which has thus far been observed and disclosed by me."

I shall offer no excuse for making copious extracts from this chapter; nor shall I enter into any argument to prove the statements true. If they do not, by their intrinsic beauty, reasonableness, benign tendency, and obvious accord with your highest conceptions of the love and wisdom of God, as well as of the grand capabilities of the human soul and the final destiny of the righteous, commend themselves to your judgment, I do not believe that any argument I could offer would have weight with you. I submit these extracts, therefore, to your candor; and leave you to judge whether they be, or be not, worthy the high origin claimed for them:

"Every one may know that man, when he leaves the external or natural, comes into the internal or spiritual man. Hence it may be known that heavenly delight is internal and spiritual, not external and natural; and because it is internal and spiritual, that it is purer and more exquisite than natural delight, and that it affects the interiors of a man which belong to his soul or spirit.

"All delights flow from love; for what a man loves, he feels to be delightful; nor is there delight from any other source. Hence it follows that such as the love is, such is the delight. The delights of the body or the flesh all flow from the love of self and the love of the world, whence also are lusts and their attendant pleasures; but the delights of the soul or spirit all flow from love to the Lord and the neighbor, whence also are the affections of good and truth, and interior satisfactions. These loves with their delights flow-in from the Lord and from heaven by an internal way, and affect the interiors.

"Heaven in itself is so full of delights, that, viewed

in itself, it is nothing but delight and blessedness; for the divine good proceeding from the Lord's divine love makes heaven both in general and in particular with every one there; and the divine love wills the salvation and happiness of all. Hence it is, that whether we speak of heaven or of heavenly joy, it is the same thing.

"The delights of heaven are ineffable and likewise innumerable. But innumerable as they are, not one can be known or believed by him who is in the mere delight of the body or the flesh; since his interiors look from heaven to the world, thus backward. For he who is altogether in the delight of the body or the flesh, or what is the same, in the love of self and the world, feels no delight but in honor, gain, and the pleasures of the body and the senses; and these so extinguish and suffocate the interior delights which belong to heaven, as to destroy all belief in their existence. Such a man therefore would greatly wonder, if he were only told that when the delights of honor and gain are removed, other delights remain; and still more if he were told that the delights of heaven which succeed in the place of them are innumerable, and of such a nature that the delights of the body and flesh, which are principally those of honor and gain, cannot be compared with them.

"How great the delight of heaven is, may appear from this circumstance alone: that it is delightful to all there to communicate their delights and blessings to each other. And because all in heaven are of this character, it is obvious how immense is the delight of heaven; for there is in heaven a communication of all with each, and of each with all. Such communication flows from the two loves of heaven, which, as was said, are love to the Lord and the neighbor; and it is the nature of these loves to communicate their delights. Love to the Lord is of this nature, because the Lord's love is the love of communicating all that He has to all his creatures, for He wills the happiness of all; and a similar love is in each of those who love Him, because the Lord is in them. Hence there is with the angels a mutual communication of their delights to each other. That love toward the neighbor is also of a similar quality, will be seen in what follows. From these considerations it is evident that it is the nature of these loves to communicate their delights.

"The man who is in love to God and his neighbor, does not, so long as he lives in the body, feel a manifest delight from these loves and from the good affections thence derived; but only a blessedness almost imperceptible, because it is stored up in his interiors, and veiled by the exteriors which belong to the body, and blunted by worldly cares. But his state is changed after death. The obscure delight and almost imperceptible blessedness which had been enjoyed by those in the world who were in love to God and the neighbor, are then turned into the delight of heaven, which becomes perceptible and sensible in all manner of ways; for that blessedness which lay stored up and hidden in their interiors when they lived in the world, is then revealed and brought forth into manifest sensation; because they are then in the spirit, and that was the delight of their spirit.

"All the delights of heaven are conjoined with uses, and are inherent in them; because uses are the goods of love and charity in which the angels are. Therefore every one has delights corresponding in quality with his use, and in degree with his love of use.

"Certain spirits, from an opinion conceived in the world, believed heavenly happiness to consist in an idle life, and in being served by others. But they were told that happiness by no means consists in mere rest from employment, because every one would then desire that others' happiness should be his own; and if every one had this desire, none would be happy. Such a life would not be active but indolent, and through indolence the faculties would become torpid; when yet they might know, that without an active life there can be no happiness, and that cessation from employment is only for the sake of recreation, that one may return with greater alacrity to the active business of his life.

"It was afterward shown by abundant evidence, that angelic life consists in performing works of charity, which are uses; and that the angels find all their happiness in use, from use and according to use. They who entertained the idea that heavenly joy consisted in living an idle life, and in breathing eternal delight without employment, were allowed to perceive the nature of such a life, in order to make them ashamed; and it was found to be extremely sad; and after a short time—all joy having departed—they felt only disgust and loathing for it.

"Some spirits who believed themselves better instructed than others, said that it was their belief in the world that heavenly joy consisted solely in praising and glorifying God; and that this was an active life. But they were told that, to praise and glorify God is not such an active life; and that God has no need of praises and glorification; but that his will is that they perform uses, that is, the good works which are called goods of charity. But they could have no idea of heavenly joy in doing the good works of charity, but an idea of servitude. The angels however testified, that in the performance of such good works there is the highest freedom, because it proceeds from interior affection, and is conjoined with ineffable delight.

"Almost all who enter the other life, suppose that every one is in the same hell, or in the same heaven; when yet there are infinite varieties and diversities in both. The hell of one is never precisely like that of another, nor is the heaven of one exactly the same as the heaven of another; just as no man, spirit or angel, is ever exactly like another, even as to the face. When I only thought that two might be exactly alike or equal, the angels were astonished, saying that every whole [*unum*] is formed by the harmonious agreement of many parts, and that the character of the whole is according to that agreement;

and that therefore every society of heaven makes a one, and all the societies of heaven collectively; and this from the Lord alone by love.

"In like manner uses in heaven are according to all variety and diversity. The use of one angel is never exactly similar to, or the same as, that of another; nor is the delight of one altogether like the delight of another. And further still, — the delights of every one's use are innumerable; and those innumerable delights are in like manner various, but yet conjoined in such order that they mutually regard each other, like the uses of every member, organ and viscus in the body; and still more like the uses of every vessel and fibre in each member, organ and viscus, each and all of which are so connected together, that every one regards its own good in another; and thus each in all and all in each. From this universal and particular regard they act as one.

"I have several times conversed with spirits who had recently come from the world, concerning the state of eternal life; remarking that it is important to know who is the Lord of the kingdom, what the nature of the government, and what its form; for, as nothing is of greater moment to those in the world who remove to another kingdom, than to know who the king is and what his character, what the nature of his government, and many other particulars relating to that kingdom, so it is of still greater importance that such knowledge be had respecting this kingdom, in which they are to live to eternity. Let them know, therefore, that the Lord is the King who governs heaven, and also the universe, — for He who governs one governs the other; thus that the kingdom wherein they now are is the Lord's, and the laws of this kingdom are eternal truths which are all based upon this law, that they love the Lord above all things and their neighbor as themselves; and still further, — if now they wished to be like the angels, — they ought to love their neighbor better than themselves.

"On hearing these things, they were unable to make any reply; because in the life of the body they had heard something of the kind, but had not believed it. They marvelled that there should be such love in heaven, and that it were possible for any one to love his neighbor more than himself. But they were informed that all goods increase immensely in the other life; and that man's life while in the body is such that he cannot go beyond loving his neighbor as himself, because he is in corporeal principles; but when these are removed the love becomes more pure, and at length angelic, which is to love the neighbor more than themselves; for in heaven it is delightful to do good to another, and not delightful to do good to one's self unless that the good may become another's, thus for the sake of another. This is to love the neighbor more than one's self.

"I have conversed with spirits who supposed heaven and heavenly joy to consist in being great; but they were told that in heaven he is greatest who is least, for he is called least who has no power and wisdom and desires to have none from himself, but from the Lord. He who is least in this sense, has the greatest happiness; and because he has the greatest happiness, it thence follows that he is the greatest; for thus he has all power from the Lord, and excels all others in wisdom. And what is it to be the greatest, except to be most happy?— for to be most happy is what the powerful seek by power, and the rich by riches. They were further told that heaven does not consist in desiring to be the least with a view to being the greatest,— for then one sighs and longs to be the greatest, — but in cordially desiring the good of others more than one's own, and in serving them for the sake of their happiness, not with any selfish regard to recompense, but from love.

"Heavenly joy itself, such as it is in its essence, cannot be described, because it is in the inmosts of the life of the angels, and thence in every particular of their thought and affection, and from these in every particular of their speech and action. It is as if their interiors were wide open and free to receive delight and blessedness, which is distributed to every single fibre, and thus throughout the whole frame. The perception and sensation of delight and blessedness thence resulting, surpass all description.

"Certain spirits were desirous to know what heavenly joy is; therefore they were allowed to perceive it to such a degree that they could bear it no longer. But still it was not angelic joy,— scarcely in the least degree angelic. This was proved by its actual communication to me, when I perceived that it was so slight as almost to partake of something rather frigid; and yet they called it most celestial, because it was their inmost joy. Hence it was manifest, not only that there are degrees of the joys of heaven, but also that the inmost joy of one scarcely approaches the ultimate or middle joy of another; also, that when any one receives that which is the inmost to him, he is in his own heavenly joy, and cannot bear a more interior degree thereof without pain.

"Almost all who enter the other life, are ignorant of the nature of heavenly blessedness, because they do not know what and of what quality internal joy is, forming their idea of it from corporeal and worldly joy and gladness. They are first conveyed to paradisiacal scenes which surpass every conception of the imagination. They now suppose that they have come into the heavenly paradise; but they are taught that this is not, in reality, heavenly happiness. It is therefore granted them to experience the interior states of joy perceptible to their inmosts. They are then brought into a state of peace even to their inmosts, when they confess that nothing of its nature can ever be expressed or conceived.

"In order that I might know what and of what nature heaven and heavenly joy are, it has been often, and for a long time, granted me by the Lord to experience its delights. I perceived that the joy and delight came as from the heart, diffusing themselves very gently through all the inmost fibres, and thence into the collections of fibres, with such an inmost sense of enjoyment, that every fibre seemed as it were nothing but joy and delight; and therefore all the perceptive and sensitive faculties in like manner seemed alive with happiness. The joy of bodily pleasures, compared with those joys, is like coarse and offensive grime, compared with the pure and sweetest aura. I observed, too, that when I wished to transfer all my delight to another, there flowed-in continually a delight more interior and full, in place of the former; and the more intensely I desired to do this, the more abundant was the influx of this delight; and this I perceived to be from the Lord.

"The inhabitants of heaven are continually advancing toward the spring-time of life; and the more thousands of years they live, the more delightful and happy is the spring to which they attain. And this goes on forever, with augmentations according to the progress and degrees of their love, charity, and faith. Those of the female sex, who have died old and worn out with age, and who have lived in faith in the Lord, in charity toward their neighbor, and in happy conjugial love with a husband, after a succession of years come more and more into the bloom of youth, and into a beauty surpassing every conception of beauty formed from that which the eye has ever seen. Goodness and charity are what mould their form, presenting it in their own likeness, and causing the beauty of charity to shine forth from every feature of the face, so that they are themselves forms of charity; and this so exactly, that the whole angel, and especially the face, seems charity itself. When this form is attentively surveyed, it is seen to be beauty ineffable, affecting with charity the very inmost life of the mind.

"In a word, to grow old in heaven is to grow young. They who have lived in love to the Lord and in charity toward the neighbor, become such forms or such beauties in the other life. All the angels are such forms, with endless variety; and of these heaven consists." — Ibid. 395-414.

THE LIFE THAT LEADS TO HEAVEN.

It was a prevalent idea in Swedenborg's day, that religion consisted chiefly if not entirely in formal acts of devotion — such as reading the Word and other religious books, repeating prayers, frequenting places of worship, singing psalms, receiving the sacrament, and the like. And those who spent most time in these exercises, were thought to be most truly religious, and pursuing the directest road to heaven. So completely had religion become divorced in thought from the common duties of every-day life!—so thoroughly driven out of the kitchen, the shop, the counting-house, the factory, the halls of legislation, and the seats of learning! But Christians are now fast coming to see that this was a great mistake; that religion has to do with the affairs of this lower world; and that there is no speedier or surer way to heaven, than through the faithful and conscientious discharge of our every-day duties,— for this is the way that angelhood is developed. And more than a hundred years ago, the seer of Stockholm wrote:

"Some people imagine that to live the life which leads to heaven, which is called spiritual life, is difficult; because they have been told that man must renounce the world, and deprive himself of what are called the lusts of the body and the flesh, and must live in a spiritual manner. By this they understand that they must reject worldly things, which consist chiefly in riches and honors; must live continually in pious meditation about God, salvation and eternal life, and spend their life in prayer and in reading the Word and books of piety. This they conceive to be renouncing the world, and living to the spirit and not to the flesh.

"But that the case is altogether otherwise I have learned by much experience, and from conversation with the angels; yea, I have learned that they who renounce the world and live in the spirit in this manner, procure to themselves a sorrowful life which is not receptive of heavenly joy; for every one's own life remains after death. But in order that man may receive the life of heaven, it is altogether necessary that he live in the world and engage in its duties and employments; and that then by moral and civil life he receive spiritual life. In no other way can spiritual life be formed in man, or his spirit be prepared for heaven; for to live an internal life and not an external one at the same time, is like dwelling in a house which has no foundation, which successively either sinks into the ground, or becomes full of chinks and breaches, or totters till it falls.

"I have been permitted to converse with some in the other life who had withdrawn themselves from the business of the world that they might live a pious and holy life; and with others also who had afflicted themselves in various ways, because they imagined that this was to renounce the world and to subdue the lusts of the flesh. But the greater portion of these, having by such austerities contracted a sorrowful life and removed themselves from the life of charity, which can only be lived in the world, cannot be associated with angels, because the life of the angels is one of gladness resulting from bliss, and consists in performing acts of goodness, which are works of charity.

"Besides, they who have led a life withdrawn from worldly affairs are possessed with the idea of their own merit, and are thence continually desirous of being admitted into heaven, and think of heavenly joy as a reward, being totally ignorant of what that joy is. And when they are admitted among the angels, and to a perception of their joy, which is without the thought of merit, and consists in active duties and services freely performed, and in the blessedness arising from the good which they thereby promote, they are astonished like persons who witness things altogether foreign to their expectation;

and because they are not receptive of that joy, they depart and associate with spirits like themselves, who have lived a similar life in the world.

"But they who have lived in outward sanctity, continually frequenting temples and there repeating prayers, and who have afflicted their souls, and at the same time have thought continually about themselves that they would be esteemed and honored above others, and at length after death be accounted saints, in the other life are not in heaven, because they have done such things for the sake of themselves. And since they have defiled divine truths by the love of self in which they have immersed them, some of them are so insane as to think themselves gods. Therefore they are in hell among those like themselves. Some are cunning and deceitful, and are in the hells of the deceitful; these are they who have performed such pious acts outwardly with art and cunning, whereby they have induced the common people to believe that a divine sanctity was in them. Of this character are many of the Roman Catholic saints, with some of whom also I have been permitted to converse; and their life was then faithfully described to me, such as it had been in the world and such as it was afterward.

"These statements are made in order that it may be known that the life which leads to heaven is not a life of retirement from the world, but of action in the world; and that a life of piety without a life of charity — which can only be acquired in the world — does not lead to heaven, but that a life of charity does; and this consists in acting sincerely and justly in every occupation, in every transaction, and in every work, from an interior, and thus from a heavenly origin; and such origin is inherent in such a life when a man acts sincerely and justly, because it is according to the divine laws. Such a life is not difficult. But a life of piety separate from a life of charity is difficult; yet this life leads away from heaven as much as it is believed to lead to it." — Ibid. 528-535.

THE NATURE OF HELL.

There has been, you know, much controversy among Christians in regard to the nature of hell and its torments. Understanding the Bible literally, as it was generally understood a hundred years ago, we must conclude that hell is a *place* rather than a *state of the heart;* — a lake of burning brimstone. And such was the generally accepted belief at the time Swedenborg wrote.

But very few nowadays believe in a hell of literal fire and brimstone. You no longer hear the old and once popular doctrine on this subject, proclaimed from the pulpit in any intelligent community. All are beginning to admit that the Scripture representations of the lot of the wicked after death are *not* to be literally interpreted; — that the kingdom of hell as well as of heaven is within the soul. Although few religious teachers pretend to tell us precisely what hell is, nearly all admit that the language of Scripture when treating of this subject, is to be regarded as figurative; and that God never created any such *place* as hell, but that this is simply a perverse and disordered state of the soul into which men bring themselves through a persistent disregard of the divine precepts and the unrestrained indulgence of their selfish loves. You yourself, in a sermon on "Future Punishment," published a year ago or more, said: "The educated Christian mind of all lands, for the last hundred years, has been changing on this subject" — *i. e.* the nature of punishment in the Hereafter.

Now what is Swedenborg's testimony? Writing more than a hundred years ago, he said:

"I have been told from heaven, and it has been proved to me by much experience likewise, that these two loves — namely, self-love and the love of the world — rule in the hells, and likewise *make* the hells; and that love to the Lord and love toward the neighbor rule in the heavens, and likewise *make* the heavens; also that the two former loves which are the loves of hell, and the two latter which are the loves of heaven, are diametrically opposite to each other.

"It is unknown in the world that self-love, in itself considered, is the love which rules in hell and makes hell with man. This being the case, I will first describe what self-love is, and then show that all evils and the falsities thence derived, spring from that love as from their fountain.

"Self-love consists in a man wishing well to himself alone, and not to others except for the sake of himself, — not even to the church, to his country, or to any human society; also in doing good to them solely for the sake of his own reputation, honor and glory; for unless he sees these in the uses which he performs for them, he says in his heart, Of what use is it? Why should I do this? What advantage will it be to me? And so he leaves the use undone. Whence it is evident that he who is in self-love, neither loves the church, nor his country, nor society, nor any use, but himself alone. He desires that the church, his country, human society and his fellow-citizens should serve him, and not that he may serve them; for he places himself above them, and them below himself. So far, therefore, as any one is in self-love, he removes himself from heaven, because from heavenly love.

"Still further: so far as any one is in heavenly love, — which consists in loving uses and good works, and in being affected with delight of heart in the performance of them for the sake of the church, his country, human society, and a fellow-citizen, — he is led by the Lord; because that is the love in which He is, and which is from Himself. But so far as any one is in self-love, which consists in performing uses and good works for the sake of himself, he is led by himself; and in proportion as any one is led by himself, he is not led by the Lord: whence also it follows, that so far as any one loves himself, he removes himself from the Divine, thus also from heaven.

"Self-love is of such a nature, too, that so far as the reins are given it, — that is, so far as external bonds are removed, which consist in fear of the law and its penalties, and of the loss of reputation, honor, gain, employment and life, — it rushes on in its mad career, until at last it not only desires to rule over the whole terrestrial globe, but also over the whole heaven, and over the Divine Himself. It knows no limit or bounds. This propensity lurks within every one who is in self-love, although it does not appear before the world, where the above-mentioned bonds restrain it.

"Picture to yourself a society of such persons, all of whom love themselves alone, and love others only so far as they make one with themselves; and you will see that their love for each other is not unlike that of robbers, who, so far as their associates act conjointly with them, embrace and call them friends; but so far as they do not act conjointly with them, and reject their domination, rush upon and cruelly slay them. If their interiors be examined, it will be found that they are full of bitter enmity toward each other, and that in heart they laugh at all justice and sincerity, and likewise at the Divine whom they reject as of no account. This may be still further manifest from the societies of such in the hells." — *Ibid.* 554-560.

That low or natural condition of the soul, then, in

which the love of self reigns supreme, is what is meant by hell. To be in this state, or under the influence of this love, is to be in hell. And to be in hell is to have hell in the soul. I am not aware that this view of the essential nature of hell was ever announced until revealed through Swedenborg.

THE FIRE OF HELL.

The Bible, moreover, speaks of "the fire of hell," and of the wicked being tormented therein. What does this mean? That their fleshly bodies will be cast into material fire, and burn there forever without having their organization or consciousness destroyed? Or does it mean a different kind of fire?—a fire belonging to the spiritual realm?—a fire that may forever burn within the soul without consuming it? Swedenborg answers the question thus:

"What is meant by the everlasting fire mentioned in the Word as the portion of those who are in hell, has hitherto been known to scarcely any one. The reason is, that people have thought materially concerning those things which are in the Word, not being acquainted with its spiritual sense. Wherefore by fire, some have understood material fire; some, torment in general; some, remorse of conscience; and some have supposed that the expression is used merely to excite terror, and thus deter men from crimes. But whoever is acquainted with the spiritual sense of the Word, may know what everlasting fire is.

"There are two origins of heat: one from the Sun of heaven, which is the Lord, and the other from the sun of the world. The heat which is from the sun of heaven, or the Lord, is spiritual heat, which in its essence is love; but the heat from the sun of the world is natural heat, which in its essence is not love, but serves spiritual heat or love for a receptacle.

"Spiritual heat with man is the heat of his life, because in its essence it is love. This heat is what is meant by fire in the Word. Love to the Lord and neighborly love is meant by heavenly fire; and self-love and the love of the world, by infernal fire.

"Infernal fire or love exists from the same origin as heavenly fire or love, namely, from the Sun of heaven, or the Lord. But it is made infernal by those who receive it. For all influx from the spiritual world varies according to its reception, or according to the forms into which it flows, just as the heat and light of the sun of the world are modified by their recipient subjects. The heat from this sun, flowing into shrubberies and beds of flowers, produces vegetation, and likewise draws forth pleasant and delicious odors; but the same heat, flowing into excrementitious and cadaverous substances, produces putrefaction, and draws forth noisome and disgusting stenches. So the light from the same sun produces, in one object, beautiful and pleasing colors; in another, ugly and disagreeable ones. The case is similar in regard to heat and light from the Sun of heaven, which is Divine Love.

"The evils originating in the loves of self and the world [when they rule supreme], are contempt of others, enmity and hostility against those who do not favor them, envy, hatred and revenge, and, as a consequence of these, savageness and cruelty. And in regard to the Divine, they consist in the denial, and thence in the contempt, mocking and reviling of the holy things belonging to the church; and after death, when man becomes a spirit, these evils are turned into anger and hatred against these holy things. And because these evils continually breathe the destruction and murder of those whom they regard as enemies, and against whom they burn with hatred and revenge, therefore it is the delight of their life to wish to destroy and kill; and when they are unable to do this, they still delight in the wish to do them mischief and harm, and vent their rage against them. These are the things which are meant by fire in the Word, where the wicked and the hells are treated of.

"The delight of doing injury is inherent in enmity, envy, hatred and revenge, which are the evils springing from the love of self, as was said above. All the hells are societies of this description. Therefore every one there cherishes hatred in his heart toward every other one; and from hatred breaks out into savage cruelties toward him, so far as he obtains the mastery. These cruelties, and the torment which they produce, are also understood by infernal fire; for they are the effects of infernal lusts." Ibid. 566-573.

APPEARANCE OF THE DEVILS.

The face is, to some extent, the index of the mind even in this world. The thoughts and emotions of the soul are more or less legibly imprinted thereon. But in the spiritual world the power of thought and feeling is so supreme, that they mould the face of every one into exact correspondence with themselves. Therefore the angels are inconceivably beautiful, because nothing but the most exalted beauty could fitly image the nobleness and exaltation of their thoughts or the sweetness and purity of their love.

If, then, this law of correspondence is so supreme and universal in the other world, — if there the form is so plastic to the spirit, that the outer is the exact image and correspondent of the inner man, — what should we expect would be the personal appearance of infernal spirits? If they are the opposite of the angels in character, their faces should reveal this fact. Accordingly, Swedenborg says:

"All the spirits in hell, when inspected in any degree of heavenly light, appear in the form of their own evil; for every one there is the effigy of his own evil, because with every one the interiors and exteriors act in unity,— the interiors exhibiting themselves visibly in the exteriors, which are the face, the body, the speech and the gestures. Thus their quality is known as soon as they are seen. In general their faces are hideous, and void of life, like corpses; in some cases they are black; in others, fiery like little torches; in others, disfigured by pimples, warts and ulcers. Their bodies also are monstrous; and their speech is like the speech of anger, hatred or revenge,— for every one speaks from his own falsity, and in a tone corresponding to his own evil. In a word, they are all of them images, each one of his own hell."

And mark, here, the unspeakable mercy of the Lord, in preventing the devils from appearing to themselves or to each other as they really are, and as they actually appear when seen in the light of heaven. For the seer adds:

"It is, however, to be observed that such is the appearance of infernal spirits when seen in the light of heaven. But among themselves they appear like men. This is of the Lord's mercy, that they may not appear as loathsome to each other as they do to the angels. But this appearance is a fallacy; for as soon as a ray of light from heaven is let in, their human forms are turned into monstrous ones, such as they are in reality as described above; for in the light of heaven everything appears as it really is."— Ibid. 553.

THE LORD DOES NOT CAST INTO HELL.

How can he?— seeing that He is Love itself. Love never desires to punish, but always to save and bless. A wise and loving father never wishes his child to suffer. He never chastises him but with a view to the child's own good. Nor does he ever turn away from him, however wayward and disobedient the child may be, nor cease his efforts to restrain him from evil and lead him to good. Much less, then, could He who is Love itself, turn away from *his* erring children, or cease to pursue them with tenderest pity and ceaseless efforts to do them good. Such, clearly, is the dictate of enlightened reason. And now let us hear the testimony of Swedenborg:

"The opinion has prevailed with some, that God turns his face away from man, rejects him and casts him into hell, and that He is angry with him on account of sin; and it is still further supposed by some that God punishes man, and brings evil upon him. In this opinion they confirm themselves from the literal sense of the Word, where such things are declared, not being aware that the spiritual sense of the Word, which explains that of the letter, is altogether different; and that hence the genuine doctrine of the church, which is according to the spiritual sense of the Word, teaches otherwise; namely, that God never turns His face away from man, never rejects him, never casts any one into hell, and is never angry.

"Every one, also, whose mind is in a state of illustration when he reads the Word, perceives this from the single consideration that God is good itself, love itself, and mercy itself; and that good itself cannot do evil to any one; nor can love itself and mercy itself cast man away from them, because it is contrary to their very essence, thus contrary to the Divine itself. Therefore they who think from an enlightened understanding when they read the Word, clearly perceive that God never turns Himself away from man; and because He never turns Himself away from him, that He deals with him from good, love and mercy; in other words, that He wills his good, that He loves him and is merciful to him. Hence also they see that the literal sense of the Word which teaches such things, conceals within itself a spiritual sense, according to which those expressions are to be explained, which, in the sense of the letter, are spoken in accommodation to the apprehension of man, and according to his first and general ideas.

"Man is the cause of his own evil, and not the Lord. Evil with man is hell with him; for whether we speak of evil or of hell, it is the same thing. Now since man is the cause of his own evil, therefore also he leads himself into hell, and not the Lord. And so far is the Lord from leading man into hell, that he delivers him from hell as far as a man does not will and love to abide in his own evil. All of man's will and love remains with him after death. He who wills and loves evil in the world, wills and loves the same evil in the other life; and then he no longer suffers himself to be withdrawn from it.

"From what has been said, it may be seen that the

Lord casts no one down to hell, but that every one casts himself down, not only while he lives in the world, but also after death when he comes among spirits.

"The Lord, from his divine essence,— which is good, love and mercy, — cannot deal in the same manner with every man, because evils and the falsities thence derived not only resist and blunt, but also reject his divine influx. Evils and the falsities thence derived are like black clouds which interpose themselves between the sun and man's eye, and take away the sunshine and serenity of the day. The sun, however, still continues in the perpetual effort to dissipate the obstructing clouds; for it is behind them and operating toward their dispersion; and in the meantime, also, transmits something of shady light to the eye through various indirect passages. It is the same in the spiritual world. There, the sun is the Lord and the divine love; and the light is the divine truth; the black clouds there, are falsities derived from evil; and the eye is the understanding. In proportion as any one in that world is in falsities derived from evil, he is encompassed by such a cloud, which is black and dense according to the degrees of his evil. From this comparison it may be seen that the Lord is constantly present with every one, but that He is received differently." — Ibid. 543–550.

MAN'S BOOK OF LIFE.

Besides our outer and visible record, seen and read of men on earth, there is an inner and invisible record which every soul makes for itself, and which only the all-seeing Eye can accurately read. Every man has a book of life, which he himself has written. Even now is each one engaged in writing that book — writing it every day and every hour, in living and inextinguishable characters.

This truth was disclosed, pictorially, to the seer of Patmos when he was "in the spirit," and saw, as he tells us, "the dead, small and great, stand before God;" and when, too, "the books were opened; and the dead were judged out of those things which were written in the books, according to their works."

Where and what is this book of life? and how is this record kept? Can it be elsewhere than in the soul itself? Or can it be aught else than the soul's own acts registered on the living and imperishable tablet of the heart? For what else but deeds and motives mould the character of our inner man? And will not every one, in the day of final adjudication, be judged according to his character? — *not* as it appears in the eyes of men, but as it stands revealed to God and the angels?

The following is Swedenborg's answer to these questions. See if it does not accord with the deepest philosophy and the highest reason.

"That man takes all his memory with him when he leaves the natural world, has been proved by many things which I have seen and heard; some of which I will relate in order.

"There were those who denied the crimes and enormities which they had committed in the world. Therefore, lest they should be believed innocent, all their deeds were discovered and recounted in order from their own memory, from their earliest age to the latest.

"There were some who had deceived others by wicked arts, and had stolen. Their tricks and thefts were enumerated in order, although many of them were known to scarcely any one in the world but themselves. They also acknowledged them, because they were made manifest as in the light, together with every thought, intention, delight and fear, which passed through their minds at the time.

"There were others who had accepted bribes and made gain of judgment. These in like manner were explored from their memory; and from it were recounted all their official misdeeds from first to last. Every particular was recalled — the amount and nature of each bribe, the time when it was offered, their state of mind and intention in accepting it, were all brought to their recollection at the same time, and visibly exhibited. And the number of their offences amounted to many hundreds. This was done in several instances.

"There was one who had made light of the evil of backbiting. I heard his backbitings and defamations recounted in order, and in the very words he had used. The persons whom he had defamed and those to whom he had defamed them were also made known. All these things were produced, and at the same time exhibited to the life; and yet every particular had been studiously concealed by him when he lived in the world. Another spirit who had deprived a relation of his inheritance by a fraudulent pretext was convicted and judged in the same way.

"In a word, all evils, villanies, robberies, artifices and deceits, are made manifest to every evil spirit, and are drawn forth from his own memory, and his guilt is established beyond a doubt. Nor is there any room for denial, because all the circumstances appear together.

"It is evident from these examples that a man carries all his memory with him into the other world; and that there is nothing, however concealed here, which is not made manifest hereafter in the presence of many; agreeably to the Lord's words: 'For there is nothing covered that shall not be revealed, neither hid that shall not be known. Therefore, whatsoever ye have spoken in darkness, shall be heard in the light; and that which ye have spoken in the ear in closets, shall be proclaimed upon the housetops.' — Luke xii. 2, 3.

"It may also be seen from the foregoing remarks, what is meant by the book of man's life spoken of in the Word, namely this: That all things — those he has done as well as those he has thought — are inscribed on the whole man, and appear as if read in a book when they are called forth from his memory, and as if seen in effigy when the spirit is viewed in the light of heaven.

"To the foregoing I will add a memorable circumstance concerning the permanence of memory after death, whereby I was confirmed in the truth that not only things in general, but also the most minute particulars which enter the memory, remain, and are never obliterated.

"I saw some books with writings in them, just like those in the world; and I was informed that they were taken from the memory of their authors, and that not one word contained in the book written by the same person when in the world, was wanting therein; and that thus the most minute circumstances may be called forth from the memory of another, even those which the man himself had forgotten in the world. The reason was also disclosed to me, which was: That man has an external and an internal memory — an external memory belonging to his natural man, and an internal memory belonging to his spiritual man; and that everything which he has thought, willed, spoken, done, also which he has heard and seen, is inscribed on his internal and spiritual memory; and that whatever is recorded thereon, is never erased, since it is inscribed at the same time on the spirit itself, and on the members of its body; and thus that the spirit is formed according to the thoughts and acts of the will.

"I am aware that these things will appear like paradoxes, and will scarcely be believed; but still they are true. Let no man imagine, therefore, that anything which he has thought within himself, and which he has done in secret, remains hidden after death; but let him be assured that every thought and deed is then laid open as in the clear light of day."— Ibid. 462, 463.

But already this Letter has exceeded the limits within which I had hoped to confine myself. I think it occupies more pages than both of Paul's Epistles to the Corinthians. And if you give to the extracts herein copied, that careful consideration which I hope you will, and which I think they deserve, I believe you will see and frankly acknowledge that, judged by the insight they evince and the spirit they breathe and the wisdom they contain, they will not suffer by comparison with anything which the great apostle to the Gentiles ever wrote.

I might easily have increased the extracts to five times their present number and length; and you would have found the same reasonableness, consistency, charity, and good common-sense pervading them all, that you find in those here given. And if such characteristics are to be accepted as among the signs of "mental aberration" or "singular hallucination," what sort of evidence, then, would be required to adequately authenticate a genuine revelation of the life beyond the grave?

I have yet a few more words to say on this subject; but must reserve them for future communications. Meanwhile I remain, as ever,

    Your Friend and Brother,   B. F. BARRETT.

V.

NEED AND TENDENCY OF HIS DISCLOSURES.

My Dear Brother: — In my last letter it was my purpose to vindicate the claim of Swedenborg to an extraordinary divine mission. I aimed to show that he was actually intromitted into the spiritual world, as he declares; and that he has, by a special divine authorization, made a truthful revelation of the grand realities of that world. And the only satisfactory way of doing this, seemed to be the one I adopted — to exhibit the character of the revelation itself by quoting liberally from various parts of the seer's report. This imposed on me the necessity of extending that letter to an unusual length. For while a man, laboring under a strange hallucination, might perhaps write coherently and sensibly on one or two points, it is, I submit, utterly inconceivable that he could, on scores of subjects, preserve the consistency and coherence, and exhibit the good solid sense that we find in the passages quoted in my last letter. Do those extracts read like the ravings of a monomaniac, or the speculations of one who delighted in the marvelous, or who wrote under a highly excited state of the imagination? On the contrary, are they not all pervaded by the rarest calmness, simplicity, and self-possession?—qualities which do not belong to highly imaginative writers, much less to those afflicted with mental hallucination.

Then, please to bear in mind, that while the seer, in many of the passages cited — such as those on the nature of the resurrection, the nature of heaven and hell, the state of children after death, the employments of heaven, the condition of the Gentiles in the Hereafter, &c. — has spoken according to the most advanced Christian thought of to-day, the views put forth are entirely contrary to the prevailing beliefs of Christendom at the time he wrote. Now, if you will examine those extracts in the light of Scripture, reason, observation, history, experience, well-authenticated facts, the principles of sound philosophy, the accepted laws of the human mind — all known truth, indeed — you will find their allegations sustained by the concurrent testimony of this cloud of witnesses.

Remember, too, that, during the whole period in which he claimed to have open intercourse with the spiritual world, he was teaching concerning what are commonly regarded as the fundamentals of the Christian religion,— the Lord, the Incarnation, Atonement, Regeneration, Faith, Charity, Life, the nature and way of salvation, etc.,— doctrines widely different from those commonly taught and accepted at that day, but in substantial if not entire agreement with the views of the most advanced thinkers of our own times, yourself among the number. No doubt you would be surprised to learn how much more closely your views upon all the essential doctrines of our religion agree with the teachings of Swedenborg, than with the popular belief of Christians a hundred years ago, or even with the written creed of the Congregational churches of to-day. This, certainly, would seem to be strong evidence that the prevailing belief of the "innocent delusion," "self-deception," or "mental hallucination," in his case, is by no means well founded. The genuine prophets of God may see and teach truths far in advance of the age in which they live; but enthusiasts, dreamers, fanatics, monomaniacs — I submit that no such work is ever given them to do.

Then look at the *practical* tendency of these disclosures. Consider what must be their legitimate fruits; how they ought to affect the lives and influence the conduct of those who believe them. And I know of no surer test of truth than this: the legitimate tendency, or effect upon character, of what is taught. If this be good, the teaching cannot be false; and if it be bad, the teaching cannot be true. For "a good tree cannot bring forth evil fruit, neither can a corrupt tree bring forth good fruit," saith the Lord. Nor can false teaching on any subject tend to purify the motives, exalt the aims, enlarge the sympathies or ennoble the life.

Now apply this test to Swedenborg's alleged disclosures of the future life. Take up any or every statement in the extracts given in my last letter, and consider its tendency — its legitimate influence upon the character of the believer. What could be more stimulating to all the nobler elements of our nature, than his delineation of the character of the angels, and his account of the nature, life and delights of heaven! By showing us how the angels live — how they think and feel and act — he shows us how we must endeavor to live if we would have the angel life unfolded in ourselves. In heaven, he says, no one thinks of living or working for himself alone, but all for the welfare and happiness of others; and that the more they seek each other's good, the more do they experience of heavenly delight. Suppose this were the deep conviction of all on earth, would not the tendency of such belief be most beneficent? He tells us that the delights of heaven spring from the faithful discharge of the duties of one's vocation, from the genuine love of being useful; and that happiness cannot be given there, apart from the disinterested love and performance of uses. Is not this a wholesome doctrine for men on earth to believe? Its obvious tendency is to lead every believer to seek some useful vocation, and endeavor to find his happiness in the patient and faithful performance of its duties. He tells us that every one takes his own character with him into the other world; and that there, by an unfailing law, he gravitates toward those whose ruling love is nearest like his own. Let this be believed, and what an inducement have we, while on earth, to deny and overcome within us the selfish loves of hell, and develop the purer loves of heaven! He tells us where and what is our book of life, and when and how it is written; — that daily and hourly is every one writing his own book on the living tablet of the soul. And is not the obvious tendency of his teaching on this subject, to make the believer most watchful over his thoughts, feelings, motives, and actions? — since these are all registered with mathematical exactness on leaves more durable than brass.

And so of all the great seer's disclosures concerning the Hereafter. Their obvious tendency is, to chasten and subdue the cravings of our lower nature, and to quicken all the nobler aspirations; to make the believer more humble, sincere, charitable, patient, self-forgetting, self-denying, self-sacrificing, — more like the heavenly Father himself in the spirit and temper of his mind, and in his unswerving devotion to the welfare of humanity. In short, their tendency is to make of earth a heaven. What higher evidence, then, could we ask, — what higher could we have, — that these disclosures were divinely authorized, and are therefore *true?*

Then the Bible, I think, clearly justifies the expectation of *some* such revelation as that which Swedenborg claims to have been authorized to make. It foretells the creation of a new heaven and a new earth; and the descent, from God out of heaven, of a magnificent city "of pure gold," with foundations "garnished with all manner of precious stones." It tells us that the Lord at his advent in the flesh, had many things to say which his disciples were not then able to bear; and it foretells another advent different from the first,—an advent "upon the clouds of heaven, with power and great glory." Who knows but all this points to the advent, or descent "from God out of heaven," of new and higher truth than the world has hitherto known?—to the dawn of a new and more glorious Era for humanity?—to the opening and revealing of new truth concerning the Lord, his Word, and the condition of things in the great Hereafter? Is it not plain, indeed, to the most superficial observer, that a New Age has already commenced? And may not the light which is everywhere breaking through the clouds of ignorance, the mists of prejudice, and the accumulations of error, and beginning to gild with its splendors the world's horizon, be but the first beams of Him at his second coming who is "the Light of the world"? May it not be — this coming through the clouds of the letter, of these higher, grander and more searching truths from out the spirit of the Word and from the realm of spirits, — the fulfilment of that predicted and long expected coming in the clouds, "with power and great glory"?

And does not reason, as well as the past history and present condition of the church, justify the same expectation? Go, ask your brethren in the ministry concerning the Hereafter. Ask them in what condition we shall find ourselves, when we shall have "shuffled off this mortal coil." Ask them if we shall still be in the human form, having power to think, reason, remember, converse and love. Ask them if the spirits of the dear departed still think of us and love us "on the shining shore." Ask whether, when we leave these mortal bodies, we shall join them in conscious visible association; be recognized and greeted by them, and recognize and greet them in return. Ask whether the distinction of sex is continued beyond the grave; whether spirits associate together like men and women, and what the law that determines their social arrangements. Ask what is the nature of heaven and hell, and what are the delights of good and of evil spirits. Ask if there be employments beyond the tomb, and what their nature and rewards. Ask Christian ministers these and a hundred similar questions, and nineteen-twentieths of them will give substantially the very answer you have given: "We do not know. Nothing has been revealed concerning the future life. We have our opinion on these subjects; but we do not, in our confessed ignorance, presume to teach others about them."

And will this be so always? Will the ministers of Christ, think you, *never* have aught but crude conjecture wherewith to answer inquiries upon themes of such deep interest? You believe there *is* a spiritual world. Is it reasonable, then, to suppose that its arcana will never be revealed? Does such presumption accord with what we know of the goodness of God, the wants of the soul, or the progress of mankind in knowledge upon all other subjects? For the last hundred years the human mind has made prodigious advances in knowledge of the physical sciences, and of the means of satisfying the wants and increasing the comforts of our natural life. The secrets of universal nature have been rapidly unfolding, and new discoveries still succeed each other almost with the rapidity of thought. And we can fix no limit to this progress in knowledge of the material universe. *There is no limit.* To suppose one, were to suppose that the Infinite may be exhausted; and to deny the indefinite enlargement or receptivity of the human mind.

Now, since the all-wise and loving Father is perpetually disclosing the secrets of nature for the benefit of his children, and since the liveliest imagination can set no bounds to the increase of physical knowledge, is it reasonable to suppose that all knowledge of the spiritual world will be forever denied to mortals? Will God vouchsafe to his rational creatures an unimaginable amount of truth concerning this world of matter, and keep the nobler world of spirit, which is to be our eternal dwelling-place, forever shrouded in darkness?

I submit, then, that whether we consult reason or revelation, we are justified in expecting, sooner or later, some such disclosures concerning the spiritual world as Swedenborg claims to have made.

You think that a revelation concerning the Hereafter could serve no good purpose, because if really made, it would not be understood by us mortals. I think you will change your opinion on this point when you read the extracts in my last letter. Others think there is no need of such a revelation; that it could only feed one's love of the marvelous, or gratify a morbid curiosity, which had better not be gratified. But is this really so?

Suppose you were a young man, intending by-and-by to emigrate to some foreign country, there to reside for the remainder of your life. Would you not desire some information about that country? Would you not wish to know something of its institutions and laws, the manners and customs of its people, their language and literature, their character and habits, their occupations and modes of life? And might not such knowledge be turned to profitable account in preparing yourself for the honorable discharge of your duties as a citizen of that country? And suppose some distinguished traveller had already been there, and had published a full account of what he heard and saw; would you think the time employed in reading his book, idly or unprofitably spent?

Now, is not the desire for some positive information concerning that country whither we are all going — going, we know not how soon — going, never to return — equally natural and equally legitimate? And is there no other use of such information than the gratification of a morbid curiosity? May it not stimulate and assist us to prepare ourselves more thoroughly for the duties and enjoyments of our future home? May not a faithful picture of life in heaven and life in hell, kindle in our hearts a deeper longing for the one and a more intense loathing of the other? If there be a connection between the present life and the life to come, may not the knowledge of *how* our life in the Hereafter is connected with our life here, be of high practical moment?

No *need* of a revelation concerning the future life? — either now, or at the time when Swedenborg wrote? Read the history of the Christian Church during his lifetime. Infidelity had well-nigh palsied her right arm; and a cold, cheerless, withering materialism was pressing like an incubus upon her vitals. Questions had been asked about the future life, which the wisest of the clergy were unable to answer. Many had come to deny, and still more to doubt, even the immortality of the soul. To arrest this infidel tendency, there was needed just such a disclosure of the realities of the other world as that made through Swedenborg; and accompanied, too, with precisely that rational kind of evidence, which alone could satisfy the demands of a reasoning and inquisitive age.

A revelation concerning the Hereafter *of no use*, even if true? Go ask that mother as she bends over the pulseless body of her beloved child, and impresses upon its marble brow the last fond tribute of a mother's love. Ask her if she could find no solace in the assured conviction that her darling is in the loving embrace of angels — more truly alive, and happier far, than ever before.

Or, ask that widowed wife, whose blood-shot eyes and pallid cheek bespeak an agony too deep for words. Ask her — while the coffin-lid is closing over the lifeless form of him to whom her affections clung with all the devotion of a woman's love — whether it would not lighten the burden of her sorrow to know something definite and positive about that realm into which her beloved has just been ushered. Ask whether it would not gladden her aching heart to *know* that he is more alive now than ever before; that his spirit is by her side, tenderly watching over her, ready to soothe her in her sorrows, and to encourage and strengthen her in every good word and work; — ready, perchance, when her earthly pilgrimage is ended, to clasp her again in love's embrace.

Or, ask that youth or maiden who stands, overwhelmed with anguish, by the bedside of a dying father, mother, sister, or brother; or that thronging crowd of mourners who weep the departure of the loved and good, and whose dark apparel is but a faint emblem of the gloom funeral which shrouds to them the spirit-land; — ask them if a truthful revelation of the grand realities of the other world would bring no comfort to their riven hearts. Ask if they would find no solace in the assured conviction that their loved ones are still alive and near and watching over them for good — inspiring holy thoughts and good resolutions and noble endeavors — fuller than ever before of life, activity, health and joy.

Or, ask the thousands who have experienced and therefore *know* the sustaining power, under sore bereavement, of the revelation that *has been* made; — who once looked on death with dread dismay, but are now able to contemplate it with a cheerful serenity, and sometimes even with a holy joy. Ask them, and they will testify to the use of this new revelation; and they can speak from a living experience. They will tell you that not the wealth of kingdoms nor the honor of thrones can be compared in value with the priceless truths concerning the spiritual world, which they have found in the writings of Swedenborg.

But lest I weary you by my prolixity, I will bring this letter abruptly to a close — reserving the remainder of what I wish to say, for another and concluding epistle, and subscribing myself, as I am, and hope ever to be,

Truly your Friend and Brother,

B. F. BARRETT.

VI.

COLLATERAL TESTIMONY.

MY DEAR BROTHER: — I have already laid before you some of the more direct evidence of Swedenborg's alleged and extraordinary intromission into the spiritual world, to wit: the intrinsic reasonableness, consistency, need and value of the disclosures he has made. If you examine this evidence with sufficient care and thoroughness, you will, I doubt not, find it of a nature that cannot easily be overthrown or invalidated. You will see that the alleged revelation itself is the very best evidence of its truth.

But there are some facts to which I have not yet alluded, which I think deserve your consideration, and which cannot fail to add strength to my argument; facts which cannot be denied, and which seem to me of great force and significance. Such, for example, as these:

That every year witnesses a more and more liberal infusion of the principles, philosophy and doctrines of Swedenborg, and the spirit of his teachings, into the best literature of our times. As one of the striking cases in illustration of this remark, I might mention the works of

George McDonald, which are all aglow with the spirit and philosophy of Swedenborg's teachings. Further:

That the changes in theological opinion which have been taking place for the last half century, and are still in progress (and you, I doubt not, will concede that important changes have occurred among the more advanced thinkers in nearly all the churches), have been and continue to be in a direct line toward the teachings of the Swedish seer; and the most popular preachers and writers on theology of to-day, are the men who have studied Swedenborg the closest, and whose teachings are most imbued with his doctrines and philosophy. To cite a single case by way of illustration, — that of Rev. E. H. Sears, author of those precious works, "Regeneration," "The Foregleams of Immortality," and "The Heart of Christ," — works which Christians of every name concede to be among the most luminous and valuable contributions to theological literature ever made by an American writer. Of the latest and last-mentioned of these works, the *Boston Congregationalist* says: "It is instructive and suggestive in the highest range of Christian thought and feeling." *The Church and State* says of it: "No book of recent American theology is likely to win more notice from thoughtful readers than this." *The Light of Home* says: "It is one of the most deeply interesting volumes of this generation." *The New York Independent* says: "'The Heart of Christ' is destined, we believe, to exert a powerful influence upon the opinions of thinking men in all branches of the Church." *The Liberal Christian* says of it: "This is certainly one of the most interesting and valuable offerings to theological and devotional literature, which has been made in our country in this generation." *The Boston Journal* says: "It is long since there has appeared in theological literature a work of such power and significance as 'The Heart of Christ.'" *The Cincinnati Times and Chronicle* says: "It is a very *vital* book, and merits the careful study of all religious readers." And other leading journals contain notices equally laudatory.

Here, then, is a work extolled as few works ever were before, — alike by orthodox and heterodox, by the secular and religious press; yet its theology and philosophy throughout are in entire agreement with the teachings of Swedenborg, — *and with no other theological system*. I doubt if there is a paragraph in the book to which the most ardent admirer of the great Swede, and devout believer in his divine illumination, would take the least exception. And I may say the same of the other two charming works by the same author. Nor does Mr. Sears attempt to conceal his profound regard for Swedenborg, or his belief in his superior illumination. Speaking of the sensuous method of interpreting the Apocalypse adopted by all other writers, he says:

"Swedenborg is the only interpreter we have ever met with, who does not flounder in this interminable slough. He keeps consistently on the spiritual plane; and though we do not pretend to understand his entire exegesis, we believe his method is the only rational one for interpreting a purely symbolical book; and that in the work under consideration [the Apocalypse], it unfolds some of the profoundest truths that ever searched the nature of man." — *The Heart of Christ*, p. 97.

Again, in the same work, he says:

" The spiritual body evolved from the natural, does not put off at once all its natural appearances and adaptations." And as a foot-note to this he adds: "Swedenborg in his very rational pneumatology illustrates this at large, showing that the changes from an earthly to a heavenly condition through death, are not made by crossing over chasms, but by the life within unfolding in an orderly way and robing itself anew, so that the natural appearances just before death and just after may be similar."— p. 401.

Again, in his " Foregleams of Immortality," referring to Swedenborg's " Divine Love and Wisdom," he says:

" It contains, among other things, a dissertation on the 'Doctrine of Degrees'; and under its peculiar terminology the reader does not at first get the pith of its philosophy. But when he does get it, he sees the amazing sweep of the principle set forth, and its constructive power in theology; and that by missing it every school of materialists has stuck fast to the earth, — Pantheism, babbling of sacred names that mean nothing, the Church glooming among the sepulchres, and modern Spiritualism offering us a future world of sublimated matter; and he sees, too, that without the key which this principle offers, they will never get out of that prison-house, but knock their heads eternally against the bars."

Not that Mr. Sears is a Swedenborgian in the popular or technical sense. I do not mean to convey any such idea; for it is not true. Besides, that would rather weaken than strengthen my argument. He is larger than any of the sects, — the Swedenborgian included; and believes that good Christians are to be found in them all, — yes, and *outside* of them all. He believes with you (as you have expressed yourself in your admirable sermon on "The Power of Love,") that "the marrow of a true religion is love;" that "the true church is the one which has in it the divine art of producing love, and that continuously;" that "a man's salvation does not depend on his creed;" that "there is in love a logic that is mightier than interpretation;" that "whether a man be high-church or low-church, new-church or no-church; whether he hold this creed or that creed or no creed, if he has this saving power of love in the soul, grace be upon him;" that "all those of every church and every faith, who love the Lord Jesus Christ and their fellow-men in sincerity, are of our fellowship — are Christ's, and are spreading Christ's kingdom." And you would find him ready to agree with you most cordially, I doubt not, when you say in that same sermon:

"And how glorious is the church of God now upon the earth! Not that narrow, contending church which the eye can see; not that church upon which you can put the arithmetic, and which you can measure; not that church whose cathedrals and buildings you can behold — not that is the church of God; but that larger church which is invisible. That is the only true church — a church wherein there is harmony — which is made up of all good men [and women]. It is that church which is made up of the concurring hearts of those who love the Lord Jesus Christ in sincerity and in truth."

With equal cordiality, too, I believe Mr. Sears would assent to the following, which forms the concluding paragraph of your excellent sermon on "The Church of the Future":

"When men would discuss with you the Church of the Future, tell them that with definite organization it will have infinite diversity. It will not be so much a temple, as a city with endless variety of structure, with uses and ornaments expressed in a hundred ways; but that in spirit it will be one; in creed one; and that creed and spirit will be, LOVE TO GOD AND LOVE TO MAN!"

And just here it may be worth your while to remember, that more than a hundred years in advance of both yourself and the author of "The Heart of Christ," the seer of Stockholm wrote, that "love to the Lord and the neighbor constitutes the essence of heaven and the church." And this in substance is repeated hundreds of times in his works. Passages like the following are among those of most frequent occurrence in his writings.

"This distinction of names [among churches] arises solely from doctrinals; and would never have existed if the members of the church had made love to the Lord and charity toward the neighbor the essential points of faith. Doctrinals would then have been only varieties of opinion concerning the mysteries of faith, which they who are true Christians would leave for every one to receive according to his conscience; while the language of their hearts would be, He is a true Christian who *lives* as a Christian, that is, as the Lord teaches. Thus one church would be formed out of all these different ones, and all disagreements arising from mere doctrinals, would vanish." — *Arcana Cœlestia,* 1799.

"Let this truth be received as a principle, that love to the Lord and charity toward the neighbor are the essentials on which hangs all the Law, and concerning which all the Prophets speak, and that consequently they are the essentials of all doctrine and of all worship, tnen all heresies would vanish; and out of many churches, however differing as to doctrinals and rituals, there would be formed one church. In this case, all would be governed as one man by the Lord; for they would be as the members and organs of one body, which, though not of similar form or function, still have relation to one heart on which they all depend, both in general and in particular, be their respective forms ever so various. In this case, too, every one would say of another, in whatever doctrine or whatever external worship he might be principled, This is my brother; I see that he worships the Lord, and that he is a good man." — Ibid. 2385.

"All the particulars of the doctrine of the New Jerusalem relate to love to the Lord and love toward the neighbor. Love to the Lord consists in trusting in the Lord and doing his commandments; and to do his commandments constitutes love toward the neighbor. That they love the Lord who do his commandments, the Lord himself teaches in John xiv. 21-24; and that love to God and love toward our neighbor are the two commandments upon which hang all the law and the prophets, see Matthew xxii. 35-40. By the law and the prophets is meant the Word in its whole complex." — *Apocalypse Revealed.*

"With those who are of the genuine, spiritual church, charity [or love] is the essential thing, or is in the first place; whereas with those in whom faith is separate from its good, both as to doctrine and life, the truth of faith is the essential thing, or is in the first place. These latter are not of that church; for life [or disinterested neighborly love] constitutes the church, but not doctrine except so far as it be of the life. Hence it is evident that the Lord's church is not here nor there, but everywhere — both within those kingdoms where the church [called Christian] is, and outside of them — where the life is formed according to the precepts of charity." — Ibid. 8152. "The societies which compose it are scattered throughout the whole world, and consist of those who are in love to the Lord and in charity toward the neighbor. These societies are not only within the church [where the Word is], but also outside of it; and taken together — [invisible they are, save to Him who looketh on the heart] they are called the Lord's church scattered and collected from the good in the whole world, which is also called a communion. This communion or church is the Lord's kingdom on earth joined to his kingdom in the heavens." — Ibid. 7396.

And it would be easy to fill a volume with extracts like these, from the writings of the great seer. How far the views here expressed are in advance of the prevailing spirit and teaching of his day, no one is more competent to judge than yourself. Indeed, the great majority of the religious teachers of our own times, have not yet attained to this high standard — this just appreciation of the real catholicity of the gospel of Christ, and this perception of what constitutes the very essence of the church.

One may, therefore, affirm with entire confidence, that it is Emanuel Swedenborg who to-day is leading the whole religious world in its grand march of progress toward clearer light, a nobler charity and a higher unity. It is Swedenborg who is instructing the people, and even the religious teachers themselves, in the higher ranges of Christian thought, to a degree beyond that of any other writer. Or rather, it is the Lord who is doing this by means of the truth revealed *through* Swedenborg. It is his writings (which are the openings of the inner sense — the revealings of the divine spirit and glory of the Word) that are achieving the stupendous revolution in Christian thought and feeling which commenced a hundred years ago, and is still in progress; a revolution which can never be turned back, but must continue to advance until, in reference to the old theologies and churches, this prediction of the King of kings, "Behold, I make all things new," shall have been completely fulfilled. Does this look as if he were the dreamer or mystic or fanatic or self-deceived enthusiast, that he is commonly reputed? Does it not look, rather, as if he were a man ordained and sent of God?

Consider, further, how the popular estimate of the value of this man's writings has changed within the last thirty — yes, within the last *five* years! This may be learned from the greatly altered tone and attitude of the periodical press, both secular and religious. Thirty years ago, the newspapers rarely mentioned him or his writings; and when they did, it was oftener in derision than otherwise. But latterly a great change has come over our most popular journals in regard to the great seer. Not only are they beginning to speak of him with respect, but they tell their readers that his writings are getting to be a power in the realm of religious thought; that they deserve to be carefully studied by our religious teachers and guides;' that no minister can longer afford to be ignorant of them.

Not long ago the *Chicago Advance* said: "Swedenborg deserves to be studied as a philosophic writer not often excelled in profundity, acuteness, variety and consistency of thought." The *New York Independent* (March, 1869) said : " Whoever desires to understand modern theology and the elements which have contributed to its formation, has need to study the writings of Emanuel Swedenborg." And three years later, the same great and truly independent paper said : " There is in Swedenborg's writings a marvelous insight — a vision of the higher truths of philosophy and religion, to which few men have attained. No Christian minister should fail to acquaint himself with the main principles of his system." And in a still more recent issue : " We have no doubt that the Church of Christ will come at length to accept with great thankfulness the large amount of truth that the writings of Swedenborg contain, and to rank him among the best of its teachers." The *New York Evening Post* says : "Certainly he who desires to understand the religious convictions of the present age, cannot afford to be ignorant of the contribution which Emanuel Swedenborg has made toward them." The *Chicago Tribune* says : " Many persons of all sects are greatly interested in Swedenborg's teachings, and it seems likely to leaven more or less the entire lump of modern religion." And the *New York Evening Mail* says : "Swedenborgianism is becoming an element of great activity and importance in the religious belief and life of to-day. It is very true, as has been observed lately by several critics, that the doctrines of the Swedish seer have become a permeating formative influence throughout the orthodox churches."

And this list of commendatory notices of the illustrious Swede and his teachings, might be largely increased from the leading journals of the last five years. I need not tell you how different all this is from the attitude of the periodical press on the same subject thirty years ago; or what a different estimate of the seer and his writings it clearly indicates. And what is the conclusion to be drawn from it? That people are losing their senses? — that they are getting more and more bewildered in theology, and in their bewilderment are ready to accept the dreams of an enthusiast or the utterances of a lunatic for revealed truth? Or is it that thinking men and women are gradually coming to see that the world's former estimate of this man and his writings, was altogether erroneous? — and that, with its progressive advancement in general intelligence and spiritual perception, it is fast coming to a truer appreciation of them? — coming to see that what it had so long looked upon as dreams or fantasies, are substantial and God-given verities? I leave you to judge.

But it is quite time to bring this letter to a close. Yet I have not said a tithe of what I might say, and should be glad to say, on this interesting and pregnant theme.

I hope you will weigh with candor the considerations I have presented; and especially that you will study carefully and prayerfully the extracts made in my last letter. I believe you will do this. And if you do, I have no doubt but you will change from the attitude assumed in your sermon on "The Hereafter," and confess yourself mistaken when you declared that God has made no revelation concerning the Future Life. I am encouraged in this belief by what I know of your rare candor and spiritual insight, as well as by the fact that you have evidently changed your view of the Divine Trinity since my letters to you on that subject, thirteen years ago. For in your sermon which was the immediate occasion of those "Letters," you declared your belief that Father, Son, and Holy Spirit, "are three beings, with separate and distinct understandings, with separate and distinct conscience, with separate and distinct will;" adding, "I understand their threefold personality as much as I understand the existence of three different friends." But ten years later, in a sermon on the Holy Spirit, you say: "The Holy Spirit pervades the universe. It is to the personality of God, what the light and heat of the sun are to the sun itself"—that is, an *effluence* or *emanation*. And this is precisely the view set forth in my Letters; for I say: "The Holy Spirit is not a *person* but an *effluence*—that divine and holy Proceeding of love and wisdom from the Lord, corresponding to the natural proceeding of heat and light from the sun." (p. 123.) Having found reasons for changing your previous view of the Trinity, I cannot doubt but you will find equally valid reasons for changing the position to which I have taken exceptions, in your recent sermon on "The Hereafter."

But I trust you will believe me when I say, that it is

not in the hope of achieving a personal victory that I write. I have no ambition of that sort that I am aware of. Still less desirous am I that you should become "a Swedenborgian," in the technical or popular sense of that word. If you should come to believe as fully as I do in Swedenborg's extraordinary illumination and special divine mission, I would not have you join the "Swedenborgian" organization, nor change in the least your present church relations. I would advise you to remain right where you are, and preach just as you are preaching, advocating and illustrating the widest fellowship, and owning no master save the Lord Jesus Christ. Whatever truth we receive is *his* truth, and is therefore to be proclaimed in his name, let it come through whatsoever channels it may.

Nevertheless I would impress upon you the seriousness of the questions you are now called to consider. They are none other than these: Did God illumine Emanuel Swedenborg after the manner and to the extent alleged? Did he open the eyes of his spirit, and thus intromit him into the spiritual world, and enable him for many years to hold open intercourse with angels and devils? And has He actually made through him a veritable revelation concerning the great Hereafter?

These are grave questions, demanding a serious answer. However shallow- or worldly-minded men may treat them, *you* cannot afford to ignore them, nor leave them unsolved. You can, if you try, answer them as well as any other man living — can answer them correctly. You can weigh the evidence and appreciate its force. But before you can come to a just decision, you must examine the revelation itself with seriousness and care; — not merely the extracts given in my last letter, but the works of the great seer himself.

For if the facts and evidence in the case be such as to compel an affirmative answer, — if a revelation of the Hereafter has indeed been vouchsafed, — the event must be reckoned as one of the most momentous in the whole history of the Church, or even of the human race. The revelation must have been granted, because seen by the all-wise and loving Father to be suited to his children's needs, and a means of drawing them nearer to Himself and the hosts of shining ones in the realms above.

After a careful and prayerful study of this alleged revelation for more than thirty years, bringing to bear upon it the best powers of my understanding and the deepest experiences of my heart, I can testify to its reasonableness, its consistency, its entire agreement with all known truth, and the immense spiritual comfort and satisfaction it is capable of ministering. When you shall have bestowed on it much less time and thoughtful study than I have, I confidently believe your testimony will agree with mine. I believe you will receive from it, or through it, a prodigious increase of spiritual power. I believe it will supply — what your preaching seems now to lack — that unwavering faith and cheering light and uplifting joy as touching the Hereafter, which can come only from positive and deep conviction.

"Watch therefore,"—to cite the Master's own words; —"for in such an hour [perchance, too, in such a *manner*] as ye think not, the Son of Man cometh.

"Who, then, is that faithful and wise servant, whom his Lord hath made ruler over his household, to give them meat in due season.

"Blessed is that servant whom his Lord, when he cometh, shall find so doing."

I add no more—save the unfeigned expression of my high esteem for you personally, and my confidence that, in reference to the subject on which I have written you, as well as to all other matters, you will act worthy of yourself and your sacred calling. This confidence I shall ever cherish, and hope ever to remain, as I am,

Your sincere Friend and Brother,

B. F. BARRETT.

THE END.

CLAXTON, REMSEN & HAFFELFINGER

HAVE RECENTLY PUBLISHED

THE NEW VIEW OF HELL; Showing its Nature, Whereabouts, Duration, and How to escape It. By B. F. Barrett. 12mo. Extra cloth. $1.00.

"A succinct and intelligible statement of his [Swedenborg's] doctrine of retribution. It contains much . . . that is profoundly true, and much that is exceedingly suggestive." — *New York Independent.*

"A book of great interest. . . . A really valuable contribution to the world's stock of religious ideas." — *New York Sun.*

"There is not a Christian man or woman in the world, who would not be benefited by the reading of this book." — *Westfield News Letter.*

"In 'The New View of Hell' is put forth one of the most striking and pregnant of Swedenborg's thoughts — that, too, whose influence on orthodoxy has been most observable." — *New York Evening Mail.*

LETTERS ON THE DIVINE TRINITY, addressed to HENRY WARD BEECHER. By B. F. Barrett. New and enlarged edition. 12mo. Extra cloth. $1.00.

This work has been received with great favor by intelligent Christians of every denomination. It contains a trenchant (but kind and friendly) criticism of Mr. Beecher's view of the Trinity, as stated in his sermon on "understanding God"; and presents with great clearness and force the New Doctrine on this subject, together with the Scriptural and rational evidence in its support.

LECTURES ON THE NEW DISPENSATION, signified by the New Jerusalem of the Apocalypse. By B. F. Barrett. 12mo. Extra cloth. $1.25.

The design of this volume is to unfold and elucidate the leading doctrines taught by Emanuel Swedenborg. And it is considered one of the best works for this purpose ever published. *The London Intellectual Repository* calls it "an admirable work for making one acquainted with the doctrines of the New Church [as taught by Swedenborg]." And *The New York Independent* says: "No Christian minister should fail to acquaint himself with the main principles of Swedenborg's system."

www.ingramcontent.com/pod-product-compliance
Lightning Source LLC
Chambersburg PA
CBHW020828190426
43197CB00037B/731